HBR Guide to
Leading Through Change

Harvard Business Review Guides

Arm yourself with the advice you need to succeed on the job, from the most trusted brand in business. Packed with how-to essentials from leading experts, the HBR Guides provide smart answers to your most pressing work challenges.

The titles include:

HBR Guide for Women at Work

HBR Guide to AI Basics for Managers

HBR Guide to Being a Great Boss

HBR Guide to Being More Productive

HBR Guide to Better Business Writing

HBR Guide to Better Mental Health at Work

HBR Guide to Building Your Business Case

HBR Guide to Buying a Small Business

HBR Guide to Changing Your Career

HBR Guide to Coaching Employees

HBR Guide to Collaborative Teams

HBR Guide to Critical Thinking

HBR Guide to Data Analytics Basics for Managers

HBR Guide to Dealing with Conflict

HBR Guide to Delivering Effective Feedback

HBR Guide to Designing Your Retirement

HBR Guide to Emotional Intelligence

HBR Guide to Executing Your Strategy

HBR Guide to
Leading Through Change

HARVARD BUSINESS REVIEW PRESS

Boston, Massachusetts

Library of Congress Cataloging-in-Publication Data

Names: Harvard Business Review Press, issuing body.
Title: HBR guide to leading through change / Harvard Business
    Review Press.
Other titles: Harvard Business Review guide to leading through change
Description: Boston, Massachusetts : Harvard Business Review Press,
    [2024] | Series: HBR guides | Includes index. |
Identifiers: LCCN 2024005399 (print) | LCCN 2024005400 (ebook) |
    ISBN 9781647826871 (paperback) | ISBN 9781647826888 (epub)
Subjects: LCSH: Leadership. | Organizational change.
Classification: LCC HD57.7 .H3918 2024 (print) | LCC HD57.7
    (ebook) | DDC 658.4/092—dc23/eng/20240506
LC record available at https://lccn.loc.gov/2024005399
LC ebook record available at https://lccn.loc.gov/2024005400

ISBN: 978-1-64782-687-1
eISBN: 978-1-64782-688-8

- Keep your team motivated, even when things go awry

- Build your own and your team's agility for the long term

SECTION THREE

Communicating Change

SECTION FOUR

Overcoming Roadblocks and Resistance to Change

Contents

SECTION FIVE

Building Your Team's Agility for the Long Term

APPENDIX

Understanding Change

CHAPTER 1

Change Is Hard. Here's How to Make It Less Painful.

by Erika Andersen

Every leader has had the experience of sharing an organizational change—a new system or process, a corporate restructure, a shift in the business model—and getting a less-than-positive response from their team. Sometimes the reaction is subtle: lowered eyes, tightened lips, silence. With a more confident or vocal team, you might get questions about whether the change is necessary,

---

Adapted from content posted on hbr.org, April 7, 2022 (product #H06Y5L).

complaints about "yet another thing to do," and lots of reasons why this just isn't a good time for a big shift.

Why is change so hard for us?

Blame our history as a species. Until the past few generations, most people's lives stayed very much the same from beginning to end: People grew up where their parents had grown up, did the work their parents had done, believed and knew the things previous generations had believed and known. Change, when it came, was generally an aberration and a danger.

But these days, the world is different. Major change happens moment to moment—economically, environmentally, sociologically, politically, and organizationally. Given all this, we need to rewire ourselves to be more comfortable with and open to change; we need to become more change-capable.

Shifting Our Mindset

I've been fascinated by change and our human response to it my whole adult life. When I founded Proteus International, a coaching, consulting, and leadership development training firm, our mission was focused on change: *We help clients clarify and move toward their hoped-for future.* That remains our mission today. And in working with clients over the years to make changes large and small in their organizations, my colleagues at Proteus and I have observed what happens when an individual embraces a proposed change: there's a simple, predictable, and powerful pattern. We've come to call this pattern the "Change Arc" (figure 1-1).

When a change is first proposed, most people immediately want to know three things: What does this

FIGURE 1-1

The Change Arc

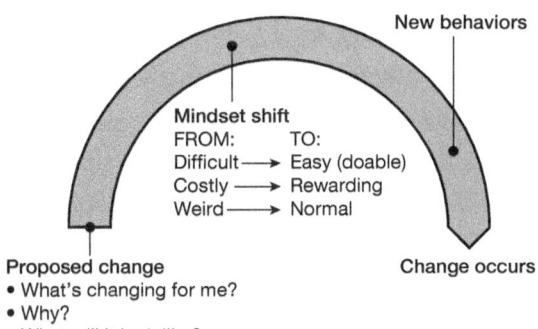

Mindset shift
FROM: TO:
Difficult ⟶ Easy (doable)
Costly ⟶ Rewarding
Weird ⟶ Normal

New behaviors

Proposed change
• What's changing for me?
• Why?
• What will it look like?

Change occurs

Source: Adapted from *Change from the Inside Out: Making You, Your Team, and Your Organization Change-Capable,* by Erika Andersen.

change mean to me, why is it happening, and what will it look like when the change has been made? We gather this information intuitively to begin to assess the level of risk and difficulty involved in the change.

As people begin to ask these questions, their initial mindset (again, based on many thousands of years of change being seen as a threat) is usually that the change will be *difficult, costly,* and *weird. Difficult* means, "I don't know how to do this, and/or other people are going to make it hard for me to do this." *Costly* means, "This will take from me things I value." This may be time or money, but is likely to involve more intrinsic and invisible valuables like identity, power, reputation, or relationships. And *weird* just means strange or unnatural: "This isn't the way we do things around here."

In observing this pattern in our clients and in ourselves, we noticed that people only begin to be open to accepting, embracing, and making a change when their mindset starts to shift from "This change is going to be difficult, costly, and weird" to "This change *could* be easy, rewarding, and normal." Once someone starts to believe that a change could be easy (or at least doable) to make, that the rewards of making the change will outweigh the costs, and that the change could become normal—that is, that it could be "the way we do things," then that person starts to be willing to operate in the new ways the change requires—they'll learn and do the new behaviors, and the change can occur.

Unfortunately, people often get "stuck" in their initial negative mindset about a change, and refuse (either quietly or overtly) to support it. And organizations and their leaders aren't very skilled at helping their people make that mindset shift. There's a well-known statistic from McKinsey & Co. that 70% of organizational change efforts fail, and that the primary reasons for that level of failure are lack of management support and employee buy-in.[1] From our observation, that lack of support and buy-in are a consequence of people staying in the "difficult, costly, and weird" mindset and not being helped to see the change in a more neutral or even positive way.

How Leaders Can Support the "Easy, Rewarding, and Normal" Mindset

So, how can you, as a leader, better support your people to make the mindset shift that will allow them to embrace change—to become more change-capable?

By using "change levers." Like physical levers, change levers are force multipliers that help accelerate people through their mindset shift around change. These are powerful tools for supporting your people through their change arc more quickly and easily, allowing changes to be adopted successfully. Here are four straightforward approaches you can take.

Increase understanding

The first thing people want is foundational information about the change. Too often, organizations communicate a change in a cheery, superficial way ("We're going to be converting to a new invoicing system—and it's great!") that doesn't provide what people need—and, in fact, can simply increase their sense of risk. It's most helpful to create and communicate a simple summary of the change that outlines:

- What it is

- Why it's happening

- The better future you'll have, post-change

For instance, instead of the superficial message above, this summary might sound like this:

We're going to be converting to a new invoicing system that's based on a platform that will work seamlessly with our current CRM. We're making this change based on feedback from both our clients and our salespeople that the current system takes too long and yields too many errors. Once we've made the transition, which

*we believe will take about four months, including
the training we'll be offering to all system users and
the behind-the-scenes work to transfer the information, invoicing will be much simpler, faster, and more
accurate.*

It's important that this summary be realistic—that
it acknowledge the time and effort the change will
require—and that it lets people know how you'll support them (with information, training, etc.) to make
the change. Once you've created this "case for change,"
expect (and be prepared to answer) questions about it.
Because we're wired to believe that most change is dangerous, we generally shift to a more neutral or positive
view only when we get the necessary information, stories, and experience to help us frame it differently.

Clarify and reinforce priorities

Letting people know what *isn't* changing as well as what
is changing can be very reassuring. Quite often, even a
major change won't have much impact on people's key
priorities.

Let's say that you're reorganizing your salesforce into
industry verticals, away from a geographic focus. By confirming that the roles and responsibilities of the account
managers, inventory and planning people, and sales
support staff will remain largely the same—and that the
overall sales goals aren't changing either—you can help
people focus on what needs to change, instead of wor-
rying about all the things that will be staying very much
the same.

CHECK YOUR CHANGE: 3 QUESTIONS TO ENSURE YOU'RE ON THE TRACK TO SUCCESS

by Ron Ashkenas

If your organization (or your piece of it) struggles with effectively implementing change, ask:

1. Do you have a common framework, language (including definitions), and set of tools (from software to checklists) for managing significant change?

2. To what extent are your plans for change integrated into your overall project plans, and not put together separately or in parallel?

3. Who is accountable for effective change management in your organization: managers or "experts" (whether from staff groups or outside the company)?

Adapted from "Change Management Needs to Change," by Ron Ashkenas, on hbr.org, April 16, 2013 (product #H00AHI).

Ron Ashkenas is a coauthor of the *Harvard Business Review Leader's Handbook* and a partner emeritus at Schaffer Consulting. His previous books include *The Boundaryless Organization*, *The GE Work-Out*, and *Simply Effective*.

So rather than saying some version of, "Don't worry, not everything is changing!" you might say something more specific to clarify the priorities: "Though we'll be reorganizing the existing sales teams to work in category verticals, and your sales goals will be industry-specific, your core priorities are still to build and maintain great client relationships while meeting your financial targets."

Give control

Especially with large-scale organizational change, employees can feel at the mercy of forces over which they have no say. By giving your people as many choices as possible during the change, you can reduce their fear and discomfort and increase the chances of engagement and buy-in.

A few years ago, we were working with a U.S.-based multinational that had just acquired a company headquartered in Latin America. The CHRO of the acquired company was worried about the change—she assumed the acquiring company would impose its systems, that she would have less influence, and that the acquirer might not understand or respect some of the HR policies necessary in her company's part of the world. She assumed the change would be difficult, costly, and weird.

Her new boss gave her control in a variety of ways. He worked with her to come up with the timing for the transition to the new systems, and he asked her to create a communication plan for how and when she wanted to announce the changes to her team. He also invited her to outline any LATAM-specific HR practices that she and her team would need to continue that weren't part of the larger company's HR processes. Giving her some elements of control in this way helped shift her mindset from negative to more supportive of the change; she began to focus on how to make the change easier and more rewarding for her team and for the rest of the acquired company's employees.

Give support

Finally, but in some ways most importantly, your people need consistent support throughout any change that affects them directly. Too often, leaders try to talk people out of what they're feeling or even just ignore it—assuming they'll eventually "get with the program."

It's critical to remember that, as a leader, by the time you communicate a change to your people, you've generally had some time to go through your own change arc. But we often expect our employees to be as accepting of the change from that first moment as we are after our own months of thought, questioning, and mindset shift.

Give them a little time to be worried, to hesitate, to ask questions, to want to know the impact on them, even to be sad or anxious. Listen. Summarize their concerns and ask what you can do to address them. Rather than labeling it "resistance," recognize they're going through the same arc you went through: They need to understand and process the proposed change and then move through their mindset shift about the change.

If you give people support in the early days of a change by listening deeply to their concerns and questions—without being dismissive or overly reassuring—they'll feel heard and supported. "You're concerned about how much time it's going to take to learn this new system," you might say, "and given all that's on our plates, that's a legitimate worry." If you take in and summarize their concerns in this way, honestly and neutrally, they'll most likely be open to hearing about the more tangible support you can offer: training, tools, demos or simulations, mentors, or affinity groups.

As a leader, if you can understand that initial fear and hesitation around change are normal, rather than assuming it means that people are "change-resistant" or "negative," and support your people through the necessary mindset shift, you'll be much better able to build a critical mass of people who will understand, accept, and adopt the change reasonably quickly. More important, you'll be helping your people to become more change-capable overall: to create skills and habits of mind to approach change in a more neutral, open way, and therefore to be better able to navigate all the changes that will arise in this new era.

Erika Andersen is the founding partner of Proteus International, a coaching, consulting, and training firm that focuses on leader readiness. In addition to her latest book, *Change from the Inside Out,* she is the author and host of *The Proteus Leader Show* podcast and the author of four previous books: *Growing Great Employees, Being Strategic, Leading So People Will Follow,* and *Be Bad First.*

NOTE

1. Boris Ewenstein, Wesley Smith, and Ashvin Sologar, "Changing Change Management," McKinsey & Company, July 1, 2015, https://www.mckinsey.com/featured-insights/leadership/changing-change-management.

CHAPTER 2

Ten Beliefs That Get in the Way of Organizational Change

by Frances X. Frei and Anne Morriss

Let's acknowledge a hard truth: A colleague you love or respect may be playing a role in unproductively lowering your organization's metabolic rate. Maybe it's even you. People often ask us about the right timing for big change, and our answer is almost always the same: How about *now*? Now is typically the right time to accelerate excellence. But first you need to address some of the common assumptions that may be holding your team back.

Adapted from content posted on hbr.org, October 24, 2023 (product #H07TP0).

1. Meaningful change happens slowly

When we view the human story from the luxury of distance, progress can take decades, generations, even centuries (or longer). History may take that long, but change can be measured in the minutes, hours, and days it takes to identify a problem and start the flywheel of action that ultimately leads to solutions. Indeed, if you look closely, history lurches forward when changemakers decide that the moment that matters most is *now*.

2. We can do it later

The most successful change leaders we know are acutely aware of the cost of not now, the high price a system pays when it's static. They live the adage that comfortable inaction is riskier than uncomfortable action. In the national reckoning on justice and race that followed George Floyd's murder, Bill Valle, CEO of Fresenius Medical Care North America, stood up and essentially said to the organization, "I don't yet know exactly what we're going to do, but I know we have to start now." He then moved quickly to empower a team to help build a stronger culture of belonging at the company.

3. Other peoples' time is an abundant, low-cost resource

If you're in a leadership role, your colleagues' time is the most strategic resource you have the privilege of consuming. The leaders who get speed right treat that resource preciously by doing everything from helping their teams to prioritize ruthlessly to carefully planning and

CHAPTER 3

The Most Successful Approaches to Leading Change

by Deborah Rowland, Michael Thorley, and Nicole Brauckmann

Management of long-term, complex, large-scale change has a reputation of not delivering the anticipated benefits. A primary reason for this is that leaders generally fail to consider how to approach change in a way that matches their intent.

Adapted from "The Most Successful Approaches to Leading Organizational Change," on hbr.org, April 20, 2023 (product #H07J54).

Consider Ling Yen*, a client of ours and finance director at an industrial manufacturing company. She sat with her leadership team, aware that the board's decision to set up a global organization for the company's specialist functions would not sit well with them. They had been through two global restructures in the last four years—with mixed success. Those changes had required endless governance reporting back to HQ, as well as tool kits and implementations that change-weary local businesses were finding only partially relevant. Ling Yen decided that she couldn't ask her people to go through that type of change again. How could she approach this change in a way that was different, sustainable, and less effortful?

When we ask leaders what they think about when deciding how to go about any major organizational change, they often struggle to answer. Too often, their attention is focused on the *what* of change—such as a new organization strategy, operating model, or acquisition integration—not the *how*—the particular way they will approach such changes. Such inattention to the how comes with the major risk that old routines will be used to get to new places.

Any unquestioned, "default" approach to change may lead to a lot of busy action, but not genuine system transformation.[1] Through our practice and research, we've identified the optimal ways to conceive, design, and implement successful organizational change.[2]

Four change approaches

Our change-approaches framework, comprising four distinct approaches to change, steers leaders through

* Names have been changed throughout.

their choices, helping them assess what model they currently use and make decisions about the optimal approach to take (see figure 3-1). This often requires a shift in leadership attitude and skill.[3]

- **Directive change:** A tightly controlled series of steps and recipes are prescribed by top management, who alone decide on the direction of the change (the what) and the way to get there (the how). There is close control over what needs to be done, change is led through marshaled programs, and buy-in is demanded. There is minimal capability building, and communications are in one-way "transmit" mode. The predominant leader mindset is "I can manage change." To Ling Yen, this sounded familiar.

- **Self-assembly change:** While top management has a clear definition of the change direction, implementation (including adaptation) is largely delegated to local management. In this approach, you see a proliferation of tools, templates, and workshops to launch change; and while these activities are closely tracked, their impact is overlooked. There might be some minimal capability building led by the tool/initiative providers (e.g., a central program management office). The predominant leader mindset is "Launch enough and something will stick." Ling Yen really felt her anxiety rising when she read this.

- **Masterful change:** Change direction is led through top management and held in a consistent manner across the organization, and leaders spend extensive time and energy on high-quality engagement and dialogue with multiple stakeholders to refine it. Within this clearly defined frame, top management gives people freedom to implement as they see fit and supports them with significant change-capability building. Formal and coordinated networks are set up to spread learning. The predominant leader mindset is "I trust my people to solve things with me." Ling Yen felt relief when considering this option ("If only!" she said).

- **Emergent change:** Leaders have a guiding intention and a loose direction, but within this expansive frame, only a few "hard rules" govern the actions of those involved in the change.[4] Rather than having a fixed, grand plan, leaders focus their action on a few hot spots and leave room for experimentation and learning from rapid feedback loops. Change moves in a step-by-step fashion, and leaders stay alert and responsive to dynamic shifts in the environment. The predominant leader mindset is "I can only create the conditions for change." Ling Yen felt that the technical complexity of her tax function could be compromised if this approach were followed, at least for now.

In four rounds of research across two decades, we've found that the two change approaches most present in successful, high-magnitude change are masterful and emergent.[5] The masterful approach was particularly present in successful long-term change, emergent in change at

2. Her team then put significant resources into discovering and understanding their stakeholders and networks, using design thinking. What did the stakeholders want and how would they like to work? How could they share the load of this complex project? "Just as the board was trusting me with a new approach, we were also trusting others. This was a revelation, and it enabled us to decide where to put our effort and where not to." Deeper understanding led her team to take further new action.

3. They then put significant investment into dedicated change skill-building initiatives, including having conversations that got beneath the surface to detect and work with systemic issues as they arose rather than after the event. They also looked at the underlying forces that would support or hinder change—for example, the company's tax function might now have to pay a price for the change.

4. They relaxed control and created a place for learning. Previously, in directive change, they had been spending inordinate time just monitoring and managing the program and not hearing about the learning that was occurring. The feedback from this approach was "No one listens to us" and "The left hand doesn't know what the right hand is doing"—in other words, people felt ignored. Now, by including stakeholders, they

created formal learning networks that regularly fed back what needed to be adjusted to make the mandated change to their function effective.

These basic changes made a large difference. While the change solution—the restructure—was set from the top, people felt more engaged and had ownership of the change. Creative ideas about how to make the model work flowed in from local geographies. The project was delivered because leaders trusted their people to solve things with them.

Emergent change in action

Another client of ours, a charity, saw its primary source of revenue drop by 47% due to the closure of its physical retail shops during the Covid-19 pandemic. Pre-pandemic, the shops had been managed regionally with a standard set of operational principles. All of this was about to change. At a critical meeting of the board of trustees, they agreed to use their volunteers as a resource. Here's how Julian, the charity head, adopted an emergent change approach:

1. Julian set a loose intention that united the whole system—in this case, halting revenue decline had become the number one priority. Emergence requires an aligning "ripe issue," yet the solution is not predetermined (as it was in Ling Yen's case).

2. It was time to experiment and use the passion and energy of the thousands of volunteers who worked with the organization. Julian's board of trustees specifically agreed that they had to create

an environment of high trust and rely on the volunteers' experience of running retail and hear their ideas. Emergent change is not a free-for-all, so they agreed that there should be a minimal set of principles (i.e., "hard rules") within which the physical retail offering could be adjusted:

- No new financial or contractual obligations.

- Retail space can be used for anything that contributes to the generation of revenue.

- Project teams post their learning on the nationwide knowledge-sharing platform.

3. Julian fostered conditions of connectivity and rapid feedback loops. Previously organized in regional pockets, technology enabled the volunteer network to collaborate at a national level. This network provided valuable insights into how retail worked as a whole. After an initial idea-generation forum, smaller networks began to form around ideas about what might halt the decline of revenue. "It was amazing," Julian said. "It felt as if we had unlocked and released a huge wave of energy that was up for anything."

4. Julian engaged the periphery and allowed differentiation. Without formal managed control but following the "hard rules," shops were now being tried and tested based on their ideas for what would work in their specific area. Differentiating ideas for urban versus rural contexts arose and

proved impactful. The volunteers had also created safe spaces for people to come and meet and learn about the charity, leading to longer-term donor relationships.

Julian perfectly summed up this approach to change: "We can only create the space and permission for change to happen—the rest is up to the others."

How to approach change

Here's how leaders can implement the change-approaches framework at their organizations:

- Start by determining your change intention. Broadly, what will the change generate? How complex will this change be? Consider its scale, time horizon, and impact on different stakeholders and areas of the organization, as well as how many variables will require change.

- Use the change-approaches framework to diagnose the current and past approaches and what might be needed now.[6] We've found masterful change to be most related to success in long-term change, and emergent change to be well-suited for when you need change to happen quickly.

- Revert to your intention. If your change requires a deep transformation in underlying beliefs and new ways of working in complex contexts, it's more than likely that a combination of masterful and emergent change approaches will be the most successful.

- If there is a gap between how you currently approach change and the approaches you most need now, investigate the underlying leadership mindsets that might need adjusting.

- Communicate your conscious decision about the change approach clearly and consistently to your organization. *How* you plan to go about the change is of equal importance to *what* the change is going to be about. Get feedback from your organization as you implement change to keep you and your team honest. Ask, "Does the way in which we go about change now feel genuinely different?" Maintain a curious approach.

- Build change literacy and capability broadly within your organization—it's not just you who needs to know about these change approaches.

The first step to being a successful change leader is to be aware of the change-implementation choices available to you. Then, make a thoughtful, intentional choice about which approach to take, and consistently hold to that choice throughout the implementation.

———————

Deborah Rowland is the coauthor of *Sustaining Change: Leadership That Works, Still Moving: How to Lead Mindful Change,* and the *Still Moving Field Guide: Change Vitality at Your Fingertips.* She has personally led change at Shell, Gucci Group, BBC Worldwide, and PepsiCo and pioneered original research in the field, accepted as a paper at the 2016 Academy of Management and the 2019 European Academy of Management. Thinkers50 Radar named her as one of the generation of management thinkers changing the world of business in 2017, and she's on the 2021 HR Most Influential Thinker list. She is a Cambridge University 1st Class Archaeology & Anthropology Graduate.

Michael Thorley is a qualified accountant, psychotherapist, executive psychological coach, and coach supervisor integrating all modalities to create a unique approach. Combining his extensive experience of running P&L accounts and developing approaches that combine "hard"-edged and "softer"-edged management approaches, he works as a nonexecutive director and adviser to many different organizations across the world that wish to generate a new perspective on change.

Nicole Brauckmann focuses on helping organizations and individuals create the conditions for successful emergent change to unfold. As an executive and consultant, she has worked to deliver large-scale complex change across different industries, including energy, engineering, financial services, media, and not-for-profit. She holds a PhD at Faculty of Philosophy, Westfaelische Wilhelms University Muenster, and spent several years on academic research and teaching at University of San Diego Business School.

NOTES

1. Deborah Rowland, *Still Moving: How to Lead Mindful Change*, 1st ed. (Hoboken, NJ: Wiley-Blackwell, 2017).

2. Malcolm Higgs and Deborah Rowland, "All Changes Great and Small: Exploring Approaches to Change and Its Leadership," *Journal of Change Management* 5 (2005): 121–151, DOI: 10.1080/14697010500082902.

3. Deborah Rowland, "Change Leaders Can Either Create Solutions or Help People Find Their Own," The London School of Economics blog, posted April 22, 2019, https://blogs.lse.ac.uk/businessreview/2019/04/22/change-leaders-can-either-create-solutions-or-help-people-find-their-own/.

4. Deborah Rowland, "Change When the Clock Is Ticking," The London School of Economics blog, posted August 6, 2019, https://blogs.lse.ac.uk/businessreview/2019/08/06/change-when-the-clock-is-ticking/; Richard Seel, "Emergence in Organisations," (2003).

5. Deborah Rowland and Malcolm Higgs, *Sustaining Change: Leadership That Works*, 1st ed. (San Francisco: Jossey-Bass, 2008).

6. Deborah Rowland, *Still Moving Field Guide: Change Vitality at Your Fingertips*, 1st ed. (Hoboken, NJ: Wiley-Blackwell, 2020).

CHAPTER 4

Six Key Levers of a Successful Organizational Transformation

by Andrew White, Michael Wheelock, Adam Canwell, and Michael Smets

Disruption used to be an exceptional event that hit an unlucky few companies—think of the old stories of Kodak, Polaroid, and BlackBerry. But in today's complex and uncertain world, as we face challenges ranging from climate change to digitization, geopolitics to DEI, organizations must treat transformation as a core capability to master, as opposed to a one-off event.

Adapted from content posted on hbr.org, May 10, 2023 (product #H07MI6).

At the same time, leaders must recognize that transformation is fraught with risk. John Kotter found in his work that 70% of organizational transformations fail, and nearly three decades later, not much has changed. Our own research, in which we spoke to more than 900 C-suite managers and more than 1,100 employees who had gone through a corporate transformation, showed similar results: 67% of leaders told us they had experienced at least one underperforming transformation in the last five years.

Considering that organizations will spend billions on transformation initiatives over the next year, a 70% failure rate equates to a significant erosion of value. What can leaders do to tilt the odds of success in their favor? To find out, we interviewed 30 leaders of transformations and surveyed more than 2,000 senior leaders and employees in 23 countries and 16 sectors. Half of our respondents had been involved in a successful transformation, while the other half had experienced an unsuccessful one.

What tactics did the leaders of successful transformations use to manage the emotional journey? To find out, we built a model to predict the likelihood that an organization will achieve its transformation KPIs based on the extent to which it exhibited 50 behaviors across 11 areas. This model revealed that behaviors in six of these areas consistently improved the odds of success. Organizations that are above average in these areas have a 73% chance of meeting or exceeding their transformation KPIs, compared with only a 28% chance for organizations that are below average. Our research suggests that any organization that can effectively implement these six levers will maximize their chances of transformation success.

Our research also found that a key difference in successful transformations was that leaders embraced their employees' emotional journey. Fifty-two percent of respondents involved in successful initiatives said their organization provided the emotional support they needed during the process "to a significant extent" (as opposed to 27% of respondents who were involved in unsuccessful transformations).

Transformations are extremely difficult on a personal level for everyone involved. In the successes we studied, leaders not only made sure their teams had the processes, resources, and technology they needed, but they also built the right emotional conditions. These leaders offered a compelling rationale driving the transformation, and they ensured that employees had the emotional support they needed to execute. This meant that when the going inevitably got tough, employees felt appropriately challenged and ultimately energized by the stress.

By contrast, leaders of the unsuccessful transformations didn't make the same emotional investment. When their teams hit the inevitable challenges, negative emotions spiked and the team entered a downward spiral. Leaders lost faith and looked to distance themselves from the project, which led employees to do the same.

The Six Key Levers of Transformations

So what tactics did the leaders of successful transformations use to manage the emotional journey? According to our research, the six levers that maximize the chances of success are:

1. Leadership's own willingness to change

Many people believe that a leader's job is to look outward and give others guidance, but our research suggests that to help their workforce navigate a transformation, leaders need to look inward first and examine their own relationship with change. "If you are not ready to change yourself, forget about changing your team and your organization," as Dr. Patrick Liew, executive chairman at GEX Ventures, told us.

In our interviews, leaders spoke of working on their own development, including engaging more with their emotions and becoming accustomed to the discomfort that accompanies personal growth. Leaders needed to "look into a mirror," as one told us, and realize that they were part of the problem before the shift to a positive trajectory could take place. They needed to remove their own fear before they could help their employees get through this change.

"As someone who was tasked to lead this [transformation], if I'm being honest with you, it was pretty unsettling at the start, because I think by nature most of us like to know the path we're going on," one COO from the automotive industry told us. And a senior vice president in the global business services industry described needing to become more vulnerable and honest on their path to self-discovery: "I think I became even more aware of myself, who I am."

2. A shared vision of success

Creating a unified vision of future success is another all-important foundation point of a transformation. In our research, 50% of respondents involved in successful transformations said the vision energized and inspired them to go the extra mile to a significant extent (as compared with 29% of respondents in low-performing transformations).

Employees must understand the urgent need to disrupt the status quo. A compelling *why* can help them navigate the inevitable challenges that will arise during a transformation program. Many of the workers who took our survey said that they "wanted" and "needed" the vision to be communicated clearly. When leaders share a clear vision, the workforce is more likely to get on board. But if people don't understand the vision or need for transformation, success is hard to achieve.

"It's not about me telling people '"This is what's going to happen,'" as a managing director in the medical device industry told us. "It's about me creating this shared sense of ownership . . . and then [coaching] my team on what they need to achieve. We very consciously want our teams to really buy into this is how we, as a collective, want to work."

3. A culture of trust and psychological safety

Trust and care from leaders can make a difficult transformation more emotionally manageable. At the most basic human level, we all know what it feels like to be seen, listened to, and heard by another person. It can validate our effort, motivate us to work harder, and help assuage emotions like doubt, fear, anger, and sadness. Workers in our study shared that they wanted leaders who were patient and who also had, in the words of one employee, a "calm and teachable spirit."

In a workplace with a high degree of psychological safety, employees feel confident that they can share their honest opinions and concerns without fear of retribution. When trust and psychological safety are missing, it's difficult to persuade your workforce to make necessary changes. For example, one senior leader told us that employees at their company were extremely fearful of the transformation and didn't feel that they could speak up about the problems they saw. Not surprisingly, the transformation did not go well.

4. A process that balances execution and exploration

Transformations obviously need disciplined project management to drive the program forward. But our research showed that leaders of successful transformations created processes that balanced the need to execute with giving employees the freedom to explore, express creativity, and let new ideas emerge. This empowers the workforce to identify solutions or opportunities that better meet the long-term goals of the transformation.

"Innovation requires the right people and processes," said one respondent to our anonymous survey. "Both are critical to encourage collaboration and experimentation."

We also found that creating space for small failures can ultimately lead to big success, whereas fear of any failure can lead to missed opportunities. Forty-eight percent of our respondents involved in successful transformations said the process was designed so that failed experimentation would not negatively impact their career or compensation to a significant extent. By contrast, only 29% of respondents in unsuccessful transformations said the same.

5. A recognition that technology carries its own emotional journey

The leaders in our study ranked technology as the biggest challenge they faced in their transformation efforts. There are a lot of emotions to manage when new systems or technology are introduced, from stress over how it works to fear about whether it will cause job loss or slow down the system.

In the underperforming transformations we studied, we saw the narrative shift away from the vision to focus on the technology itself. Whereas in the successful transformations, leaders ensured that technology was seen as the means to achieve the strategic vision. Furthermore, they prioritized quick implementations of new technology, focusing on a minimum viable product rather than perfect implementation. Finally, they invested resources into skill development to ensure the workforce was ready to create value using the new technology.

"There were kickoff sessions with our senior managers to bring them in at the beginning of the process," a vice president of a company in the media/advertising industry explained. "These sessions aimed to show them that what was being built was something that they had helped design, rather than something that was presented to them as a fait accompli. . . . This minimized the numbers of active detractors."

6. A shared sense of ownership over the outcome

In the successful transformations we studied, leaders and employees worked together to co-create an environment where everyone felt a shared sense of ownership over the transformation vision and outcome.

A prime example of this is many companies' rapid shift to virtual and remote working during the pandemic. Because of the speed and urgency of the change, leaders needed to collaborate closely with the workforce to create new ways of working and be much more responsive to their views on what was or wasn't going well. This mass co-creation helped build a sense of pride and shared ownership across both leadership and the workforce.

"In a transformation, things pop up all the time," as Christiane Wijsen, head of corporate strategy at Boehringer Ingelheim, told us. "When you have a movement around you, supporters will buffer it and tweak it each time. When you don't have this movement, then you're alone."

To conclude, it's worth reiterating that all transformations are tough. Even during successful programs, there will come a time where people start to feel stressed.

The skill at this difficult stage is being able to energize your workforce and turn that heightened pressure into something productive, as opposed to letting the transformation spiral downward into pessimism and underperformance.

What we saw throughout our research is that leaders who are truly working with their employees are much more successful. They acknowledge and manage emotions, rather than pushing them aside or ignoring them. The best leaders create vision across the organization and a safe environment to work together and listen to each other.

"You've got to be very, very respectful of people at a working level," as Thomas Sebastian, CEO of London Market Joint Venture at DXC Technology, told us. "You've got to understand the emotional side and consider a completely different perspective, such as how is this transformation going to make their life easier."

Success begets success. Once a workforce has undergone a successful transformation, they will be ready to go again. And given the pace of change in the world, organizations have got to be ready to go again.

Author's note (May 31, 2023): The authors would like to thank Debi Brannan, Zhibo Qiu, Bhavnik Mittal, Ryan Gavin, and Andres Cardona Jaramillo for their contributions to this article.

Andrew White is a senior fellow in management practice at Saïd Business School, University of Oxford, where he directs the advanced management and leadership program and conducts research into leadership and transformation. He is also a coach for CEOs and their senior teams.

Michael Wheelock leads a primary research and advanced analytics team in EY Knowledge. His team designs and delivers global mixed-methods research programs to support EY's flagship thought leadership.

Adam Canwell is head of EY's global leadership consulting practice. Adam has published extensively on leadership and strategic change. Adam has sold and delivered transformation programs across multiple industries in both the UK and Australia, working with FTSE 100 (or their equivalent) organizations.

Michael Smets is a professor of management at Saïd Business School, University of Oxford. His work focuses on leadership, transformation, and institutional change.

Implementing Change

CHAPTER 5

Help Your Team Be Open to Change

by Edith Onderick-Harvey

Leaders at every level need to embrace and model how to engage in and affect change. Having a workforce that's ready and able to harness that change will make the difference between success and failure. Personal leadership and engagement, however, is not enough. For change to be operationalized, you need to inspire your team to be creative and enable them to innovate. But innovation happens only when people are able to work in the gray space—where ambiguity is OK and business principles, rather than hard-and-fast rules, apply.

Here are five daily practices you can put in place to inspire and enable your team to become changemakers:

Adapted from "5 Ways to Help Your Team Be Open to Change," on hbr.org, April 3, 2019 (product #H04VGM).

Tell stories about others who moved beyond the status quo.

Asking people to work in the gray space often creates uncertainty. They need reassurance that moving into uncertainty can create positive results. Success stories provide tangible, memorable examples of what moving beyond the status quo looks like. To craft a compelling story, ask yourself:

- What is meaningful and important to the people I'm working with now?

- What is the core idea I want them to take away?

- What essential parts of the story invite them to come along on the journey?

For example, early in my career, I was leading a part of a project that aimed to transform the patient care delivery model in a hospital. To design key parts of the new delivery model, we were asking a cross-section of staff to work in design teams. This had never been asked of them before, and they were nervous. We gathered the 50 people together in the hospital auditorium to introduce them to the project and their role in it. I knew they were anxious about what was being asked of them, so we closed the kickoff with a scene from *Dead Poet's Society* where Robin Williams asks his students to stand on their desks and see the world differently. The scene ends with Williams telling a student, "Don't think that I don't know this assignment scares the hell out of you." Afterward, a nurse walked up to me and said, "How did you know that is me?" We talked, and I shared my confidence in how much her knowledge and experience were going to help her with this task. She went on to be one of the highest contributors to the design effort.

Ultimately, your stories should share a common message: It's OK to step up and out. Powerful stories create psychological safety, letting people know that making change is good and will be rewarded. Share how the individual(s) in the story, as well as the company, benefited from stepping into the gray space.

Create dialogue, inviting others to ask questions and share emotions, experiences, and insights.

Change stirs up emotional responses that often cause people to pull back rather than to lean in. Inspiring and enabling your team to affect change requires having conversations that move people from reaction to action. Try having 30-minute meetings to discuss both the emotions related to change and the actions participants can take to affect change. I call these "listening posts." Listening posts were originally facilities that monitored radio and microwave signals to analyze their content. Like that original definition, your listening post can help you understand key information and can help others take action. Listening posts consist of:

- **Table setting:** Define the purpose of the meeting for your team. Encourage them to discuss how change is affecting them. For example, "We're here to talk about the change we are experiencing and understand how it's impacting you personally and us as a team." Invite everyone to define actions that the group will take to influence how change is happening.

- **Listening:** Encourage individuals to start the conversation by sharing their experiences, using metaphors or adjectives. This gives them a safe way to talk about emotions. Share your metaphor first to break the ice. For example, you may feel like a juggler trying to keep all the balls in the air. Share that with your team. As people share their metaphors, remember to listen for who is dissenting or significantly challenged by the change. The voice of the outlier can provide key insights.

- **Consolidating:** Ask the team what common themes they are hearing. Use questions like, "What does it seem like we all have in common?" "What is different for each of us?" Summarize key themes and confirm what you've heard.

- **Acting:** Identify actions. These ideas need to come from the team, with you as the facilitator. Ask questions like, "What do we control or can we influence?" "How do we want to change this?" "What role will each of you play in making this happen?"

Ask "what if?" questions in one-on-one and team meetings.

This is your opportunity to help your team be bold. Don't ask what-ifs that look only at slightly different solutions or behaviors. Role-model testing the boundaries—what are the guardrails, and how can you push up against them? Questions like "What if we were all freelancers? How would we think about this?" "What if we built this process from scratch?" or "What if our lead product suddenly became obsolete?" push people to think boldly. People may be unsure just how far they can push at first. Recognize and reward initial steps, and continue to ask for more. Reinforce ideas by saying "That's a great idea. Let's push that idea even further." Or "That's a good start. We need to be asking ourselves these questions continually." This will reinforce the message that being a change maker should be the norm, not the exception.

Set expectations that everyone (including you) should acknowledge, and take responsibility for mistakes. Then treat mistakes as opportunities for learning and growth.

Michael Alter, former president at SurePayroll, made making and acknowledging mistakes a core to operationalizing business strategy. When he joined the company, he needed employees to become changemakers and take more risks to meet accelerated growth goals. After trying personal stories, analogies, and other techniques without enough success, he formalized failure. He created the "Best New Mistakes" competition, rewarding employees for providing the most unique and interesting mistakes. Rules included that employees could only nominate themselves and it had to be a new mistake. Entries were discussed, and prizes were given at company meetings. Six years later, it was still one of their most innovative learning initiatives.

Champion cross-boundary collaboration and networks to open up thinking and gain new perspectives.

To become changemakers, your team needs to hear a variety of voices and get a variety of perspectives. Urge them to work across boundaries by asking questions like:

- Who else do we need to involve?

- What other parts of the organization could help with this?

- Who has perspective on this topic/issue/area that we don't or can't have?

- How should we connect with them?

- What can I do to help create that connection?

Organizations that succeed are no longer the ones that change top-down, or where innovation is expected only from certain people or roles. Winning teams build change agility into the heart of their culture. That's why change leadership is no longer just something you do. It's a large part of who you are. And that means building "change muscle memory" in yourself and your teams. These five everyday practices are a great way to start.

Edith Onderick-Harvey is a managing partner at Next-Bridge Consulting, an organization change and leadership development consulting firm focused on helping clients stay ahead of the curve. She is a widely recognized consultant, speaker, and author who has helped clients embrace change for over 25 years. Edith is the author of *Getting Real: Strategies for Leadership in Today's Innovation-Hungry, Time-Strapped, Multi-Tasking World of Work.*

CHAPTER 6

How to Get Your Team on Board with a Major Change

by Deborah Rowland, Nicole Brauckmann, and Michael Thorley

George, head of the Asia-Pacific region for a global industry leader, was running the annual meeting of his group's 300 executives and managers. After reviewing the year to date and addressing the changing context for the coming year, he was heading for the usual wrap-up. This time, however, he had a key decision to share with

---

Adapted from content posted on hbr.org, August 4, 2022 (product #H075WO).

his people, a decision, he told us, he felt both resolute in and nervous to share. Their operating model—the model that everybody knew and understood and that guided every interaction—needed to change.

George backed up his decision by explaining that the current model wasn't working well in supporting increased customer centricity: "The model that has served us well will not serve us well moving forward, and it's dead," he told his team. He could immediately see the reactions, ranging from curious interest to mild and more severe shock. "What do you mean, it's dead?" "Who do we interface with now?" "You're disconnecting us from each other!" "What will that mean for our roles?"

George's story, one of 77 harvested from our recent round of global research into the effective leadership of change, was not atypical.[1] Moreover, the anticipation of a significant economic downturn resulting from post-pandemic developments and geopolitical conflict suggest that many executives will find themselves in restructuring situations over the next 12 to 18 months.[2] Clearly, organizations will continue to face disruptive, complex, and (probably at least in part) painful change. Has this turbulent era taught us anything about how such change should be led?

How Change Threatens Our Need to Belong

Most change management has shifted from a simplistic, top-down, "create a vision, change the structure, roll out the new program, and get buy-in" approach to more emergent, empowered, and purpose-led approaches.

But leading big, complex change is still a struggle— the rate of failure for transformation projects remains stubbornly high. Notwithstanding new agile methods, many of our clients still wish that their change efforts could go a little faster, encounter less pushback, and produce more novel and sustainable outcomes. So, what's missing?

We've seen both in our research and our work with clients that the missing ingredient is the ability to look for and work with deeper systemic forces. In every organization, unconscious dynamics exert a powerful pull on organizational behavior and effectiveness.[3] Just as gravity invisibly propels matter, these forces drive collective behavior and therefore change effectiveness. And we've found the force that has the greatest impact on change outcomes is our primary need to belong.

While "belonging" in the diversity, equity, and inclusion context—the desired emotional outcome in an organization in which each individual is invited to be fully themselves in community with others, with no parts of themselves hidden—is essential to making change happen, in the context of our research, "belonging" refers to the survival-based belonging that enables any human infant to make it to adulthood and any human adult to fully function in collective settings they give loyalty to and receive identity from.[4] Change will always threaten this kind of belonging and challenge its dearly held loyalties.

In our research, the top 12% of effective change stories featured leaders who paid significant attention to belonging. What does such attention mean? Intriguingly, we found it meant leading with two counterintuitive moves. On the one hand, these leaders took great care and time to make others feel secure, involved, and attached to meaningful work (think, "In this transformation, no one gets left behind," "You are important to me; I need you in order to make this work").

On the other hand, these leaders also recognized that change requires "un-belonging," which means two things:

- Building others' capacity to detach from past loyalties (to ways of working, to team configurations, to assumptions that no longer suit new contexts)

- Being able to stand at a distance from any strong belief group in order to allow novel solutions to emerge

So, excessive belonging impedes new futures.

Four Ways to Drive Change Through Belonging

George not only needed to persuade his team to belong to a new organizational model—he also had to foster unbelonging by unhooking them sensitively yet firmly from the existing setup while resisting any temptation to side with points of view he used to hold dear himself, which at times felt as strong as betrayal.

So how, exactly, can change leaders walk this belonging/un-belonging tightrope and skillfully attend to people's most primal need to feel secure in disruptive contexts?[5] How can they foster both loyalty and the capacity to walk away from what no longer serves? Here are four strategies.

Be mindful of your own emotions

Amid the turmoil, George took the time to look inside himself and realized that he, too, was feeling bitter about having to give up a model that had worked well for him— in other words, his own sense of belonging was threatened.[6] This physiologically impacts the prefrontal cortex as the seat of decision making and the ability to move from reactive impulse ("I'm betraying their trust!") to intentional and creative response ("This is what I know is needed to ensure our future").[7]

This neurochemical disruption influences executive function: our capacity to make decisions, process information, and plan. That's why it's vital for leaders to master a skill we call "being before doing": tuning into and regulating one's own mental and emotional reactions to experiences. When we intentionally bring our attention to the present moment—for example, by focusing on our breathing—we increase our awareness of all that is going on in and around us without immediate judgment. This preserves our thinking and decision-making abilities, stops our brains from reacting impulsively, and opens the opportunity to assess different options.[8]

Identify what people are seeking to preserve— and why

George had also learned about the vital skill of systemic perception—understanding that what you see is a symptom of deeper issues—and listened closely to the regionally structured team. He told us, "I had three teams come to me independently wanting to present, and essentially, they were presenting all the good stuff they had been doing, how they're working, all their successes. The underlying message was 'we're a really neat little team, and don't break us up.'" He realized that his people couldn't come up with the required alternative organizational design because they were almost as attached to their old teams as to family, and breaking them up seemed too painful.

Look beyond what seems like resistance to or an inability to change and perceive what people treasure and protect. It will enable you to address and challenge deep loyalties with insight and respect.

Lead difficult conversations

Once George noticed this dynamic, he addressed it in conversations with his employees: "Rather than saying 'don't break us up,' why don't we have a conversation about why you feel uncomfortable about being broken up?" This was a powerful intervention that enabled people to see their loyalty for what it was: a sentiment that was impeding the company's successful step into a more viable, product-based, global organization. Despite the difficulty of the conversation, once these attachments were named, his team felt able to "un-belong" and move into a different future. In George's words: "There was energy, enthusiasm; people settled in their new space and so it really got going. They had moved from their old roles into the new roles, and then they were working out what stuff gets done where in the new world." Truth-telling had set them free.

To help your team see not only what needs to change but why it needs to change, you have to lead conversations that explore their discomfort and help them see that as a necessary change companion.

Consider the prize and the price of change

No big change comes without a price tag. And because they're human, leaders tend to overestimate the benefits and downplay the costs. When you name and work with both, you can build true belonging, not false loyalty.[9]

By setting the context of the organizational redesign and its impact on the whole business and vulnerably admitting to his own sense of loss and bitterness, George enabled the team to see that while for them it meant losing valued intimate connections, their sacrifice would benefit the business as a whole.

Attending to un-belonging—both your own as well as your employees'—is a key element of successfully stewarding change. This will be a critical skill in the coming months as the dynamic global environment forces businesses to adapt.

———————

Deborah Rowland is the coauthor of *Sustaining Change: Leadership That Works, Still Moving: How to Lead Mindful Change,* and the *Still Moving Field Guide: Change Vitality at Your Fingertips.* She has personally led change at Shell, Gucci Group, BBC Worldwide, and PepsiCo and pioneered original research in the field, accepted as a paper at the 2016 Academy of Management and the 2019 European Academy of Management. Thinkers50 Radar named her as one of the generation of management thinkers changing the world of business in 2017, and she's on the 2021 HR Most Influential Thinker list. She is a Cambridge University 1st Class Archaeology & Anthropology Graduate.

Nicole Brauckmann focuses on helping organizations and individuals create the conditions for successful emergent change to unfold. As an executive and consultant, she has worked to deliver large-scale complex change across different industries, including energy, engineering, financial services, media, and not-for-profit. She holds a PhD at Faculty of Philosophy, Westfaelische Wilhelms University Muenster, and spent several years on academic research and teaching at University of San Diego Business School.

Michael Thorley is a qualified accountant, psychotherapist, executive psychological coach, and coach supervisor integrating all modalities to create a unique approach. Combining his extensive experience of running P&L accounts and developing approaches that combine "hard"-edged and "softer"-edged management approaches, he works as a nonexecutive director and advisor to many different organizations across the world that wish to generate a new perspective on change.

NOTES

1. Deborah Rowland and Paul Pivcevic, "Leading Change Post Pandemic: Belonging," The London School of Economics and Science blog, posted April 8, 2022, https://blogs.lse.ac.uk/businessreview/2022/04/08/leading-change-post-pandemic/.

2. International Monetary Fund, "War Sets Back the Global Recovery," April 2022, https://www.imf.org/en/Publications/WEO/Issues/2022/04/19/world-economic-outlook-april-2022; Chris Metinko, "Tech Layoffs and Hiring Freezes Appear to Accelerate," *Crunchbase News*, May 12, 2022, https://news.crunchbase.com/business/layoffs-hiring-freezes-cameo-uber-facebook-thrasio/.

3. Deborah Rowland, *Still Moving: How to Lead Mindful Change*, 1st ed. (Hoboken, NJ: Wiley-Blackwell, 2017).

4. Jena McGregor, "First There Was 'Diversity.' Then 'Inclusion.' Now HR Wants Everyone to Feel Like They 'Belong,'" *Washington Post*, December 30, 2019, https://www.washingtonpost.com/business/2019/12/30/first-there-was-diversity-then-inclusion-now-hr-wants-everyone-feel-like-they-belong/; Harriet Over, "The Origins of Belonging: Social Motivation in Infants and Young Children," *Philosophical Transactions of the Royal Society of London. Series B, Biological Sciences* 371, no. 1686 (January 2016), DOI: 10.1098/rstb.2015.0072.

5. Julianne Holt-Lunstad, "Social Connection as a Public Health Issue: The Evidence and a Systemic Framework for Prioritizing the 'Social' in Social Determinants of Health," *Annual Review of Public Health* 43, no.1 (2022): 193–213, https://www.annualreviews.org/doi/abs/10.1146/annurev-publhealth-052020-110732.

6. Deborah Rowland and Nicole Brauckmann, "Being Before Doing: Leading Disruption Starts by Turning Inward," The London School of Economics and Science blog, April 15, 2020, https://blogs.lse.ac.uk/businessreview/2020/04/15/being-before-doing-leading-disruption-starts-by-turning-inward/.

7. Junchol Park and Bita Moghaddam, "Impact of Anxiety on Prefrontal Cortex Encoding of Cognitive Flexibility," *Neuroscience* 345 (March 2017): 193–202, DOI: 10.1016/j.neuroscience.2016.06.013.

8. Adele Diamond and Daphne S. Ling, "Conclusions About Interventions, Programs, and Approaches for Improving Executive Functions That Appear Justified and Those That, Despite Much Hype, Do Not," *Developmental Cognitive Neuroscience* 18 (2016): 34–48, https://doi.org/10.1016/j.dcn.2015.11.005.

9. Rowland and Pivcevic, "Leading Change Post Pandemic;" Deborah Rowland, *Still Moving Field Guide: Change Vitality at Your Fingertips* (Hoboken, NJ: Wiley-Blackwell, 2020).

CHAPTER 7

Get Employee Buy-In

by Andrea Belk Olson

Most advice about building internal support for organizational change reiterates perfunctory platitudes, reminding leaders to communicate reasons for the change, or even to be excited about the change themselves. But in working with hundreds of companies going through organization change, I've learned that this approach is simply not enough. In fact, research shows that this narrow approach often results in a wave of employee cynicism, doubt, distrust, and negativity, which can relegate change efforts to a slow and painful death.[1]

Adapted from "Getting Employee Buy-In for Organizational Change," on hbr.org, February 6, 2023 (product #H07H2K).

What too many leaders fail to realize is that, while a certain level of skepticism to change is natural, heading it off from the start is the only way to counter it. But how?

Six Considerations to Create a Culture of Change

The most successful organizations I've worked with create a culture of change acceptance—far before they intend to introduce any changes. They do this by addressing six components of culture: legitimacy, ownership, relevance, attainability, authenticity, and impartiality. Here's how it works.

Legitimacy: Engage your organizational change influencers

When introducing change, organizations typically rely on their leadership teams, overlooking those individuals who may not hold a leadership title but are key influencers of company culture. Whether they are middle managers, key sales personnel, or even the office receptionist, these people can make or break your plan. Why? Because unlike those in traditional leadership roles, these informal influencers wield more power to shape organizational change acceptance, often through intelligence, networking abilities, or simply the respect they hold within company ranks.

Folding in those influencers early into the change process will not only build confidence across the organization via trusted yet informal leaders, but also establish a foundation for change rooted in reliable voices.

Ownership: Provide everyone a table stake

I'll say this directly: An open mic at a town hall meeting after you've decided what will be done does not amount to input. What's more, your employees likely know that you're not taking their suggestions seriously. Holding these meetings likely actually hurts your change initiative.

Instead, research shows that when people have actual agency in shaping a change, they are significantly more likely to embrace it.[2] Instead of unidirectional town halls, hold a series of small interactive discussions where departments can determine potential roadblocks and define how the change can come to life for their area of responsibility. This provides them a way to tailor execution to fit their own unique circumstances, conditions, and restraints.

Relevance: Focus on latent change

Organizations have two types of change: one they are championing today and others on the perpetual back burner, too unwieldy, complex, or politicized to tackle. While it feels counterintuitive, incorporating this second group can be the easiest way to increase buy-in for the first.

If a current change effort can be tied to other changes that have been festering and never addressed, you're in for a win. Coupling components of known needs to today's change reframes the change as crucial and integral, rather than just extra work on the pile. Further, it reinforces that leadership recognizes chronic frontline challenges and doesn't simply brush them under the rug.

Attainability: Create a series of micro-changes

The flip side of the above advice is to make sure your change is attainable. Often, change can be viewed as insurmountable due to its perceived magnitude. For instance, an IT department may have a deeply complex and intertwined technological infrastructure, limiting its ability to see the change as anything but intrusive, upending, or even catastrophic.

A useful approach in many cases is to break change efforts into a series of micro-changes. Any segmentation approach that enables change to be more digestible, achievable, and manageable will help reduce resistance by making progress attainable in the short term, while establishing a sense of accomplishment for the long term.

Authenticity: Embody behaviors that support the change

Logos, posters, stickers, T-shirts, and other swag—they're all fodder for supposedly building buy-in and excitement. But just like a dog whistle, people know what these things signal and are prepared to lie in wait until the initial excitement passes and things return to status quo.

Instead of glossing change over with superficial gifts, represent through action what the change embodies. For example, if a change focus is toward "giving more back to our community," translate it into direct behaviors, from paid volunteer hours to employee donation matching. When companies provide behavioral illustrations of what the change represents, it transforms from something stated to something acted on.

Impartiality: Establish a neutral change facilitator

Finally, be prepared for conflict. When the role of change is led solely by the CEO or C-suite leadership, individual concerns and questions get funneled to direct supervisors. Then, as conflicts between departments arise, teams jockey to have their opinion or perspective favored over another, whether it's beneficial to the larger change or not.

Bringing in a third party can help neutralize internal office politics, posturing, and infighting. This can be a trusted consultant or veteran industry expert, but ideally someone from outside the organization. Serving as part moderator, part engagement manager, and part counselor, they are there to keep decisions unbiased and eliminate favoritism.

What Happens When Employees Buy In to Change?

Although change is never easy, how leaders approach it makes a significant difference to whether it's embraced or rejected. Addressing the organizational buy-in context makes it much easier to move past resistance and stagnation, because your path forward will be shaped by realities rather than banalities. Having employees buy in to change doesn't simply make implementation easier, but rather forges an immutable and reciprocal relationship which pays infinite dividends. Without this, future endeavors will require reengaging all over again, perpetuating the cycle of resistance. Remember, trust takes months to build and only seconds to break.

Andrea Belk Olson is a differentiation strategist, speaker, author, and customer-centricity expert. She is the CEO of Pragmadik, a behavioral-science-driven change agency, and has served as an outside consultant for EY and McKinsey. She is the author of three books, a four-time ADDY award winner, and contributing author for *Entrepreneur, Rotman Management, Chief Executive,* and *INC* magazines.

NOTES

1. American Psychological Association, "Change at Work Linked to Employee Stress, Distrust and Intent to Quit, New Survey Finds," press release, May 24, 2017, https://www.apa.org/news/press/releases/2017/05/employee-stress.

2. Carolyn Dewar and Scott Keller, "The Irrational Side of Change Management," *McKinsey Quarterly*, April 1, 2009, https://www.mckinsey.com/capabilities/people-and-organizational-performance/our-insights/the-irrational-side-of-change-management.

CHAPTER 8

Build Trust on Your Team

by Amy Jen Su

Trust is a frequently used word. Just in the last month, consider how many times you've used it in thinking about your team:

- If I felt more *trust* in her, I'd give her more responsibility.

- One of the goals for our retreat is to build *trust* among employees.

- It's important that other groups in the organization *trust* my team.

Adapted from "Do You Really Trust Your Team? (And Do They Trust You?)," on hbr.org, December 16, 2019 (product #H05BTN).

While we talk a lot about trust, what do we really mean when we make these statements? Why does building trust matter so much? And what can we do as leaders to increase trust on our teams?

The *why* part may be easier to answer. Much has been written about trust and its importance in determining employee engagement, team alignment, and how comfortable a leader is delegating to others.

As to the *what and how* parts, trust can be frustrating to analyze in that it tends to be a gut feeling for us instead of a concrete choice. This makes it difficult to pinpoint the reasons why we trust one person more than another—and easy to believe there is little we can do to change that. But when we assume that trust is dependent entirely on the behavior of other people, as opposed to our own responses and interactions with those behaviors, we end up falling short as leaders.

To create work environments in which trust can flourish, we first need to understand how it really works: the various ways it can be given, built, and broken. Once we do, we can teach ourselves how to act (and react) in ways that help it grow, even in the most challenging situations, like leading a major change. The following questions are designed to help you single out the types of trust that are most lacking between you and your team. If you find that certain areas are especially weak, try taking the suggested steps to strengthen them. You might find that you also help your employees build their capabilities and characters along the way.

Trust in Performance

The first three questions address the "harder" aspects of trust: performance-based factors that have a major impact on how you and your team deliver results, make decisions, and show up to the rest of the business.

How much do I trust my team members to follow through?

At its most basic level, trust is about the work that needs to get done. To trust someone means to be confident that they will follow through on their responsibilities. I have seen whole teams fail to gain alignment and come to a screeching halt because there is an unspoken annoyance toward one person whom others consider unreliable. This typically occurs when that person isn't holding themselves, or being held, accountable, and it can take place at any level, regardless of title.

As someone in a position of power, you can prevent this. If you want your people to be more dependable and trust one another—as well as you—create an environment that encourages open communication. Here are a few ways to do that:

- **Hold regular one-on-one meetings.** Ask team members to bring a dashboard/catalog of their work. This ensures that part of the time is spent on the important items and not just on fire drills. If they are falling behind in a way that creates risk, encourage them to tell you (and don't shame them). People need to feel safe telling you about their problems, or you won't be able to help resolve them. Sometimes this may mean taking some things off their plate or reprioritizing. Other times it may mean clearing obstacles that are holding them back.

- **Be fair when giving feedback.** Set clear standards for assessing performance at the start of a project. When giving feedback during your one-on-ones, make sure you do so equally based on the standards you originally set. This way, everyone will know what is expected of them and be held mutually accountable for their actions.

- **Approach those who may be struggling silently.** Some team members may not feel comfortable approaching you with a problem. Signs that someone may be having a hard time include: demotivation, lack of productivity, high stress, or trouble focusing.

How much do I trust my team members to bring good judgment?

When you find yourself getting burned out as a result of overinvolvement in other people's projects or because every decision must be approved by you, it's a sign that you need to work on your ability to give trust in this area. By holding trust back, you not only create process restraints for your team, you risk essentially saying to them, "I don't trust you to do good work without me."

There are a few ways you can change your leadership style to rebuild trust in this situation:

- **Good judgment is a muscle—help your team build it.** After making important decisions, talk them through with your team. Explain the subjective and objective criteria you considered, risks and trade-offs you assessed, and stakeholder considerations. This will teach people how and why you make the choices that you do, give them a better understanding of the company's priorities, and demonstrate the factors you would like them to consider when making judgment calls in the future.

- **Acknowledge that failure will happen, and that's OK.** Consider the mistakes you've made in your career and how they've helped you grow into the leader you are today. Give your team that same space. Let them flourish and fail. And when they fail, help them grow from it as opposed to writing them off. This means letting them make big or hard decisions on their own from time to time. Wean yourself out of situations where you can bear a little risk. You can always follow up with people after and highlight areas for improvement.

- **When a team member makes a poor judgment call, be curious, not dismissive.** Ask them guiding questions to push their thinking and deepen your understanding of their thought process: What assumptions or criteria underlie your assessment or decision? What risk framework did you apply to this? How will this impact the budget, timing, or work for another group? If they are unable to answer those questions, ask them to come back to you with more information or data to back their argument. Ultimately, this dialogue will allow you to more accurately assess your team member's judgment capabilities and lead you both to a better solution down the line.

How much do I trust team members to represent me and the organization?

Your decision to offer team members greater visibility, both internally and externally, is typically drawn from how well you think they will inspire the confidence of key constituencies. This includes showing up with a professional presence, displaying confidence, and being able to engage with others effectively.

If you're hesitant to give certain employees this opportunity, consider why. At the end of the day, your lack of trust could be keeping them from growing and reaching their full potential. To build trust in this area, try doing the following:

- **Set your employees up for success.** Sometimes people don't know the expectations your organization has for engaging professionally with others, and when this happens, it is no wonder they fall short. Prepare them by creating a set of principles outlining the ways in which they should engage with key constituencies within and outside the company. Explain what your function's value proposition is and how that should be communicated to others.

- **Provide coaching and mentoring opportunities to those interested or those who show potential.** One way to do this is to invite team members to observe or participate in executive meetings or presentations with you. As you watch their skills grow, you will not only be building their confidence, but also growing their trust in you as a mentor, and your trust in them as a performer.

- **Be clear about who serves as the point person for important contacts.** The more exposure your team members get, the more opportunity there is for confusion to arise around who owns what relationships. Let your team know whether or not you are delegating full relationship ownership to them. If you're not, then discuss the best ways to tag-team the relationship and keep each other in the loop. This way, you can empower people without feeling like they are stepping on your toes.

Trust in Principles

The second three questions address "softer" aspects of trust: principle-based factors that have real impact on your team's engagement and satisfaction, as well as the perceived integrity of your team by those with whom they work.

How much do I trust my team members to practice an appropriate level of discretion?

Because knowledge sharing and "being in the know" are powerful ways to connect with others, it can be challenging for people to decipher which information is most useful to share and which information is best kept private. More often than not, this is why people unintentionally breach confidences.

But trust in this area is so important. When you start overediting yourself due to a lack of confidence in your team's discretion, you risk holding back information that will help them do their jobs well, and their performance can suffer as a result. There are some things you can to do to build a strong foundation of trust in this case:

- **Educate your team.** Let them know from day one that not everything you share internally is free game, particularly information that is protected by NDA or creates a conflict of interest with another party or key customers. Provide them with examples of exactly what you mean so they can easily recognize and avoid dangerous situations. If you share something sensitive during a meeting and you want it kept private, don't assume people can read your mind. Just say so.

- **Set ground rules.** Let people know that any personal information that is shared by a team member within team time together should be treated respectfully. By setting these standards from the start, you will be showing your team that you respect their privacy and take it seriously. Further, you will be helping to build a culture of trust, and they will be more likely to value the privacy of others and the organization at large when necessary.

- **Be an accessible resource.** If your direct reports are unsure about grey areas, especially during times of change or uncertainty, advise them to come to you or HR for counsel. It's important for people to know you are available to support them.

Do I trust my team members to respect the psychological safety of others?

Our brains are trained to constantly scan for and avoid people who threaten our sense of well-being.[1] When we perceive someone who is a "threat," we either attack or retreat, and when we retreat, we lose access to important skills such as listening, asking questions, or speaking up about our ideas. This is why it's so important to maintain a positive team culture. If people feel psychologically unsafe due to one bad egg, they likely won't reach their full potential.

If there is a lack of psychological safety on your team, use the following steps to build (or rebuild) it:

- **Model healthy conflict.** When you and a team member have a disagreement, whether in a one-on-one or in a larger meeting, approach it respectfully by giving the other person space to voice their point of view. It's important that you welcome and acknowledge opinions that are different than your own—even if it means engaging in civil debate. Doing so shows the rest of your team that it's possible to share opposing perspectives with a tone and approach that is constructive.

- **Have zero tolerance for bullying.** If you witness a team member engaging in blatantly rude behavior such as interrupting, dismissing, steamrolling, condescending to, or using derogatory language toward others, address it immediately. Almost every team I have worked with has, at one point or another, had a toxic member who impacts the camaraderie and collaboration of the group. Rather than avoiding the elephant in the room or forcing everyone to work around that person, you, as the leader, must hold them accountable for their behavior, even if they are a strong performer.

- **Create a culture of appreciation.** Reinforce and capitalize on each person's strengths, perspectives, and contributions to the team by calling out their achievements and wins in meetings or group settings. A culture that focuses only on negative feedback or what people are doing wrong can leave your team feeling discouraged or defensive.

How much do I trust my team members' underlying intentions and motivations?

Ultimately, we need our teams to work toward doing what's best for the organization. This can be tricky, as personal motivations are often at play and our assessment of them can either increase or decrease our trust in others.

While you can't control a person's intentions, there are things you can do to encourage and reward team play:

- **Break down silos.** Try to manage less by "hub and spoke." Instead, be intentional about activities that build esprit de corps. Remind people that they are part of a larger collective by creating shared team goals and connecting them to the bigger picture. Explain how each person's work influences the performance of the larger organization.

- **Consider that people may not be the problem.** Sometimes performance management and incentive systems are the real issue. Ask yourself: Do our compensation systems only reward individual contributions? Is there anywhere in the performance management system where we can applaud or address team players?

- **Be willing to have a direct conversation.** Don't reward bad behavior. If someone is overly self-absorbed, explain that they are hurting, not helping, themselves. Remind them that leadership roles require cross-functional and team collaboration and that their success will be determined, in part, by how well they work with others.

As you continue to think about how to increase trust among your team and the best ways to create an environment in which it can flourish, return to these six questions. In time, you may find that you are able to more quickly identify pain points that you can help resolve or strengthen. When you give trust, you not only empower others, you also develop the individuals on your team into stronger contributors and, in doing so, you empower yourself as a leader.

––––––––––

Amy Jen Su is a cofounder and managing partner of Paravis Partners, a premier executive coaching and leadership development firm. For the past two decades, she has coached CEOs, executives, and rising stars in organizations. She is the author of the HBR Press book *The Leader You Want to Be: Five Essential Principles for Bringing Out Your Best Self—Every Day* and coauthor of *Own the Room: Discover Your Signature Voice to Master Your Leadership Presence* with Muriel Maignan Wilkins.

NOTE

1. David Rock, "Managing with the Brain in Mind," *Strategy + Business,* August 27, 2009, https://www.strategy-business.com/article/09306.

CHAPTER 9

When You Have to Carry Out a Decision You Disagree With

by Art Markman

One of the great frustrations of being a middle manager is that senior leaders make decisions that go against what you would have done had it been up to you. Sometimes you are part of the decision process, and other times the decision is simply handed down. Either way, you are now responsible for ensuring that the plan is carried out.

Adapted from content posted on hbr.org, February 9, 2018 (product #H045FJ).

A natural reaction in this situation is to begrudgingly go along with the chosen course of action. You might even be tempted to communicate to your peers and supervisees that you're not convinced this is the right way to go.

Check your level of trust

Resist that temptation. Your job is to help your organization succeed. You won't be fulfilling that role if you—intentionally or unintentionally—undermine the decision. Instead, start by asking yourself whether you trust the organization you work for. If, deep down, you don't feel that senior management makes good decisions, it's probably time to start looking for another job.

But if you *do* trust the organization, then begin by convincing yourself that the decision is actually a good one. This is what I did early in my academic career when I received peer review comments on a paper I'd submitted for publication. Without fail, there would be at least one reviewer who hated the paper. They did not get the point of my argument, or they had reservations about the studies I had done.

When this first started happening, I hated those reviewers and assumed they hadn't read my paper carefully. Eventually, though, after I served as a reviewer on enough papers to realize that the authors whose papers I was reviewing probably wanted to dismiss my comments as well, I began to trust that the reviewers had valid points. Perhaps those points reflected my own bad writing, or (perish the thought), perhaps my experiments were not as brilliant as I thought they were. Ultimately, trusting that they had valid points made my papers better.

Take the decision-makers' perspective

To convince yourself of the validity of the decision, put yourself in the shoes of someone who believes deeply in it. Ask yourself why someone would make this choice. Look for factors you may not have considered before that would make this option a good one. While you're at it, also be explicit about all of your objections. Those will be useful as well.

Move forward

Once you've wrapped your head around why this decision was reasonable, you're ready to start working with your team to carry out the new plan.

This approach helps you—and your team—in two ways.

First, how much effort your team puts into making a plan succeed depends in large part on how much they believe in it. If you communicate a new course of action halfheartedly, you'll get less than peak effort because people will sense that you're not enthralled with the job to be done.

Also, even the best plans run into some difficulties for a variety of reasons: The plan might be failing, more effort might be required, or the team needs to innovate to find the right way to implement it. How the people you work with interpret inevitable problems and what's required to remedy the situation depends on their commitment to the plan. If, picking up on your trepidation, they're already looking for reasons why the option will fail, they are much less likely to be motivated by difficulties they face than if they believe deeply that the plan will succeed. Communicating a plan with confidence can help create a self-fulfilling prophecy.

Second, the reservations you have about the decision can strengthen the plans you develop with your team. That list of objections you made when convincing yourself the plan is a good one comes in handy here: It reflects your beliefs about the potential obstacles to success. You are already aware of some of the reasons why the plan could fail. Use this list of obstacles to develop contingencies to handle what you think can go wrong. Research suggests that the better prepared you are for problems before they happen, the better able you'll be to handle them when they arise.[1]

Finally, teach this method of dealing with disappointing decisions to the people who work for you. When you move up in the organization, you are likely to make decisions that fly in the face of what some of the people believe is right. You want them to treat your choices with enough respect to give them the best chance to succeed.

———

Art Markman is the Annabel Irion Worsham Centennial Professor of Psychology and Marketing at the University of Texas at Austin and founding director of the program in the Human Dimensions of Organizations. He has written over 150 scholarly papers on topics including reasoning, decision-making, and motivation. His most recent book is *Bring Your Brain to Work: Using Cognitive Science to Get a Job, Do It Well, and Advance Your Career* (Harvard Business Review Press, 2019).

NOTE

1. Peter M. Gollwitzer, "Implementation Intentions: Strong Effects of Simple Plans," *American Psychologist* 54, no. 7 (July 1999): 493–503.

Communicating Change

CHAPTER 10

How to Tell Your Team That Organizational Change Is Coming

by Liz Kislik

From time to time, every leader has to deliver news that is hard for employees to hear. Even when businesses are doing well, organizational and structural change is to be expected, and acquisitions, reorganizations, policy changes, or technological advancements can affect people's jobs in ways that create feelings of fear, anger, or sorrow. Each employee wonders, "How will this change

---

Adapted from content posted on hbr.org, August 9, 2018 (product #H04HEL).

affect me?" or assumes, "Oh, this won't be good! How am I going to get my work done?"

Announcements like these can be daunting. And they go awry if the message is insufficiently planned or poorly delivered. But by attending to the following crucial components, leaders can be ready to communicate the news in ways that will help recipients adjust well, recover quickly, and move forward to execute the change.

Plan more time than you ever thought necessary to prepare the content, the delivery, and the necessary follow-up.

Typically, you should expect to hold not just one initial "all hands" meeting or videoconference, but also a series of smaller team and individual conversations as follow-ups. As one of my clients was going through a series of organizational changes, a valued middle manager reacted negatively in each town hall, asking inappropriately detailed questions, as if it were a game of "gotcha," to show that the ramifications hadn't been fully considered. Once his boss made clear that he would have the opportunity for continuing formal and informal discussions, the manager kept himself in check and was able to offer specific suggestions to improve implementation.

Also, take pains to coordinate announcements so that no one is caught flat-footed if the news is being released at different intervals by individual managers and organization-wide outlets. It may feel like you're overinvesting in planning, but it will save you time and pain in the long run. Giving people multiple opportunities to take in and process the announcement is essential for thorough understanding; receiving the information from the right sources in the right sequence is crucial for credibility.

Equip all levels of management to explain the context.

Provide training and rehearsal or role-play time to everyone who will need to communicate the message; don't assume they'll have the right instincts. Otherwise, to escape their own discomfort, they may dump the news or blame management, either directly or indirectly.

One client's executive team had to do significant repair when frontline managers announced to their teams that there would be a cutback in bonuses because "they said you didn't do enough," rather than explaining the reasons for the results and the plans already under way to improve those results for the future. Employees who had worked as hard as they could were frustrated and resentful, and distrusted senior management for some time thereafter.

Describe the organizational pain and how the new solution alleviates it.

Instead of just announcing a disruptive change, give the background of what's not working today and why the new plan is the best way to get to the desired outcome. Focus on how customers have been hurt, how the business is incurring extra expense, the negative brand impact—and how the change will help mitigate those problems. When one client had to consolidate multiple operations to increase efficiency and reduce time to market, it was clear that there wouldn't be room for all the incumbent leaders. It helped to review the shared history and the acknowledged pain points.

Personalize both the impact and the resolution.

If you don't, employees may not understand which specifics apply to them, or even how the company is providing support or services to help them cope. For example, in the small group or individual meetings, come prepared with all the necessary details to be able to answer personal questions immediately, rather than creating even more anxiety and aggravation while you assign someone to work out the specifics you didn't research in advance. When one client changed its health plans to keep costs down, it helped covered employees research their doctors' eligibility and find new practitioners when necessary. The employees were grateful for the individual attention and support and were subsequently less resentful even though items such as deductibles and copays had gotten more expensive.

Give the affected people as many options and as much participation as you can.

When they have choices—and the necessary information or support to make them—employees feel more respected and maintain more pride and autonomy. The closer people are to the work, the more likely it is that they'll generate practical ideas. At one organization that was having some financial difficulties, we facilitated a series of meetings about cost-cutting measures that let everyone look for ways to help out—even though they were adversely affected by some of the very measures they proposed.

And don't assume you know what's best for each individual or what they might choose. When a client company was absorbed into a larger operating unit, some deeply committed HR executives stayed till the bitter end, providing outplacement for their colleagues despite knowing that by the time they looked for jobs themselves, the best opportunities would already have been filled.

Demonstrate humility and responsibility, not just authority.

Many leaders mistakenly believe that they'll be given a pass for shaking up people's lives if they say they're suffering over the decision or the disruption themselves. Even treating the problem as a shared responsibility can backfire and feel manipulative to employees. Instead, say things like, "I'm sorry I didn't anticipate . . . " or, "I was too enthusiastic about x . . . " to show that you take seriously the impact of the situation on others. You can't prepare for every curveball, so if you don't have the answer to a question, say something like, "Wow, that's a question we didn't think about, but it's a good one. We'll get back to everyone with an answer early next week." Don't try to fake your way through.

You can use this kind of planned approach to ensure that news of your organization's change is heard, recognizing that different people will perceive information differently. It can feel unnecessarily painstaking to take the time to plan and then work through all the details with your employees.

SPEAK CONFIDENTLY—EVEN DURING CHAOTIC TIMES

by Darcy Eikenberg

"The chaos right now in our organization is overwhelming," Lara revealed during our executive coaching session. Her company had just hired a new CEO, and the ripple effects of change were traveling throughout the organization. "I need to keep my team focused and encouraged, but anything I say feels fake and distracting. Should I just stay quiet until things calm down?"

When I speak with managers like Lara, I know she's not alone in wondering what to say to her team. We're taught that our people require more communication during tough times, and yet we worry that sharing our honest observations will backfire.

Staying silent might seem like a safer approach. However, it only generates what INSEAD professor Nathan Furr calls "unproductive uncertainty," where nothing moves forward. While we wish we could hit pause and wait for the confusion to clear, we know that moment may never arrive.

Here are two ways to think differently about what you say, so you can speak confidently to your team no matter what.

Recognize the power of "and." One verbal tool is to use the word "and" more intentionally. This allows you to align two seemingly separate thoughts—things are difficult, and things will be OK. For example:

- "We're making fantastic progress on our main project, and the new COO is considering changing the direction of that work. We'll continue to focus on our progress and trust in our experience that we'll adapt if we need to."

- "Our team's been struggling while Mara's out on maternity leave, and this gives us a chance to rethink those processes and requirements."

- "The supplier is a month behind schedule, and so we can shift our attention to project Y."

Using "and" more frequently ensures you're not over-indexing on the good out of fear of making your team worry about the bad. Your people are smart—they know nothing can be perfect, and they'll welcome the truth.

Teach the past to arm the future. In most businesses, we aspire to move forward quickly and not dwell on the past. But reminding your team about times when they—and the company—thrived unleashes evidence that you can succeed again. You can use your company and team's history, whether you lived it personally or not. Here are examples my clients have used:

- "Many of you are new here, and may not remember when we went through the last recession.

(continued)

SPEAK CONFIDENTLY—EVEN DURING CHAOTIC TIMES

Here are a few things that happened then and how we worked through them."

- "Angela, I'm betting you recall our challenges before, during, and after the last acquisition like the one we're managing now. Would you share a few stories with us?"

- "While I'm still new to the company, I'm not new in our field. If it's helpful, here's what I learned during the last time I experienced this kind of change."

Even if your team comprises new hires, there's history behind why the work exists and the pain or problem it solves. Unpacking the past and connecting it to the present helps you create more certainty in the future.

When you are able to communicate with confidence, your team will be better able to address their concerns and feel in more control of their work, even amid changes, setbacks, and stressors.

Darcy Eikenberg is an executive coach and leadership speaker who teaches leaders how to help their people stay. She's the author of *Red Cape Rescue: Save Your Career Without Leaving Your Job* and writes regularly at RedCapeRevolution.com.

Adapted from "How to Speak Confidently to Your Team During Chaotic Times," on hbr.org, August 25, 2023 (product #H07S3M).

But knowing you've done everything you could to help them withstand challenges and move ahead will make it much more satisfying when you finally achieve the desired results.

Liz Kislik helps organizations from the *Fortune* 500 to national nonprofits and family-run businesses solve their thorniest problems. She has taught at NYU and Hofstra University, and has spoken at TEDxBaylorSchool. You can receive her free guide, *How to Resolve Interpersonal Conflicts in the Workplace,* on her website, lizkislik.com.

CHAPTER 11

Communicate Clearly During Change

by Elsbeth Johnson

A former colleague liked to remind leaders of their impact by telling them, "There are children you've never met who know your name." The point was simple: Their followers were also moms or dads who were going home and talking about their day in front of their children. And you, their leader, had a starring role in that story. As leaders, we are far more visible than we think, and we are sending signals to followers all the time—even when we don't realize it.

Adapted from "How to Communicate Clearly During Organizational Change," on hbr.org, June 13, 2017 (product #H03PQF).

And while sending the right signals to our followers is important at any time, it is especially important during times of strategic change, when followers are trying to make sense of a new "ask" from the organization, in the context of all the existing asks they are grappling with.

Why, then, is it so hard for leaders to send clear, effective signals to followers?

In my experience of working with leaders, and in my research which asks followers what they need from leaders during times of change, there are three main ways in which leaders often confuse their organizations with the signals they send. Get these signals right, and you set people up to respond and deliver the change you've asked for; fail to signal clearly and effectively in these three ways, and you'll have confusion at best—and at worst, the opposite of the strategic changes you've asked for.

Signal No. 1: Telling your organization what you want

You'd think this would be the easy bit, but the evidence suggests that this is where leaders most shortchange their organizations. Too many followers tasked with delivering strategic change report that their leaders weren't clear enough about what they wanted the change to achieve or about what it would entail.

It seems the reasons for this are twofold: Leaders too often express what they want in terms not of *outcomes*, but of *tasks*, and they rarely, if ever, make clear the full *extent* of the change they are asking for.

One client I worked with recently—let's call it Sales and Product Co.—was trying to make its business more customer-centric. Its leaders had expressed what they wanted as a list of activities that their middle managers would be asked to work on. There were nine projects. The list gave middle managers clarity about what to do, certainly, but it told them nothing about why they were doing it, or how their myriad activities might fit together to create a cohesive program. So we worked with them to re-express what they wanted as outcome-level targets. "Conduct exit interviews with all departing customers" became "Reduce the customer attrition rate," for example. A target to improve cross-selling rates through more outbound calls per month became simply "Improve profit per customer."

And because the middle managers now knew the targets outcomes leaders wanted, within weeks they were able to identify better, smarter, and cheaper ways to deliver them. Instead of nine projects, they settled on just two: this drove alignment across activities as well as accountability for them. And because the two were chosen by people close to the business who understood the interactions of customer data and processes far better than the senior management team could (or should), the projects had a far better chance of delivering their outcomes. When asked why they knew it was these particular two projects they should work on, the middle managers said, "Well, we knew what the outcomes had to be. And we know how the business works, so it's not that hard." The importance of specifying outcomes for followers, rather than choosing activities for them, was clear.

Why is this signal so hard to get right?

Leadership teams I've worked with have an almost primal urge to give their middle managers a list of activities.

It makes them feel like action is being taken and that they are helping their hard-pressed middle managers by telling them exactly what to do. It's also much easier to jump from "We need to change" to "Here's what to do" than it is to thrash out the difficult trade-offs involved.

Left to their own devices, many leadership teams shortchange the questions of what they want the change to achieve, and why. When we work with leaders, we often have to push them to continue thinking about these questions and to answer them with sufficient clarity. But even as we do, we regularly have someone in the leadership team come up to us in a coffee break and say something along the lines of, "So, all this is great, but when are we going to *get down to it*? You know, talk about what we're actually going to *do*." It usually takes several conversations, and stubbornness, to help them see that this is what they as leaders needed to "get down to"—and, conversely, that until this is done, any scoping out of activities is premature.

In particular, there are four questions that senior teams often skate through too quickly:

1. **Why do we need to change, and why now?**
   What are the imperatives driving this change? Why is the previous strategy no longer good enough? Where on the P&L are we feeling, or anticipating, pain? Are you sure you want X to change, even if it means you can't have Y anymore?

2. **What is the full extent of the change we need?**
   Don't underestimate the extent of the change

you need, either privately or publicly. However tempting it is to tell people that this is just an incremental change—when it is nothing of the sort—or however politically expedient it seems to underplay the extent of the change required, a lack of clarity about the extent of the change will make subsequent conversations about resources and priorities much harder.

3. **If we figure out 1 and 2, what should improve as a result? How will we measure the improvement we've been targeting?** And perhaps most overlooked of all . . .

4. **How does this new strategy or change link to previous strategies?** Answering this question is critical if leaders are to reduce the confusion that a cumulative overload of strategic or change initiatives—another year, another "strategy"—and their potentially conflicting targets can cause. If leaders can't explain these links clearly, then you need to revisit the need for this change (questions 1–3) or phase out some of the existing initiatives.

Once you have sufficiently clear answers to these four questions, you have the first ingredient for successful signaling.

Signal No. 2: Personally living the change you've asked for

Living the change you want to see means much more than modeling any behaviors you've asked for; it also means making a myriad of decisions that support the change. It is what David Nadler and Michael Tushman called "mundane behaviors" in their exploration of how change becomes institutionalized.[1] It means changing how you spend your time. How you choose to use your most precious, finite resource (your own diary) is a critically important signal you send as a leader. If you're not giving time to the change you've asked for, followers will interpret this to mean that the latest change is not really being important, and will act accordingly. For Sales and Product Co., this meant the C-suite routinely scheduling time to discuss progress and leaving enough space in their diaries to be available to discuss issues and blockages as the need arose.

It also means changing the agenda of senior team meetings and board discussions. For Sales and Product Co., this meant putting "customers" literally at the top of the agenda for every senior team meeting. Before this seemingly tiny change, the C-suite had talked about customer issues after sales, products, and regulation, and just ahead of "any other business." This order had often meant that customer issues didn't get discussed at all, or were rushed through by tired execs eager to close the meeting. In an organization that sought to become more customer-focused, this couldn't go on. Talking about customers early in every meeting gave them the priority and attention they deserved. It also meant that never again would followers ask their C-suite exec, "What did you discuss at the board meeting?" to hear the answer "We didn't get to the customer stuff."

Why is this signal so hard to get right?

Two reasons. It's partly because carving out time, and making sure you always have spare time in your diary for strategic issues as they arise, is always harder than it sounds. You may also have to make this time available for years ahead, given how long strategic change takes to embed. That means having to say no to a lot of other people and their priorities if you are to keep time available for this priority.

And there will be many times when your old, "usual" issues will feel like such urgent priorities that you will be tempted to get them out of the way first, before turning your attention to the more important "strategic" stuff. This is a trap. Sort out the most important issue first—and sort it properly. Your business will then be in fundamentally better shape on the urgent issues.

But the second reason why personally living the change is a hard signal to send is that it's effectively a full-time job. Managing yourself—day in and day out, even when you don't feel like it—is hard. One of the leaders I've worked with describes this as "an out-of-body experience," where he is trying to be simultaneously in the moment with someone, listening to them and thinking about the issue, and also *external to himself*, deliberate about how he is showing up and conscious of the impact he is having on those around him. Like all mundane behaviors, it is very easy to not notice that you are not doing them—and that, of course, is precisely when your followers are looking most closely at you.

Signal No. 3: Resourcing and measuring the change you've asked for

How your organization spends its resources (capital, people, capabilities) and what it chooses to measure are the final critical ways it signals what is important. As a leader, you disproportionately shape these decisions, and therefore the clarity of these signals. This means finding the resources needed to deliver the change you've asked for. It doesn't just mean money—though that is important. It also means allocating the right people, with the right level of seniority, experience, and political connections, to work on the change. These are all ways you can signal to the organization that the change is important.

It also means making changes to what you measure, and making them early on. All too often, a new change spends its first few quarters being undermeasured because the existing suite of metrics the organization uses haven't been overhauled to reflect the new priorities. If what gets measured is what gets managed, give the change its best chance by signaling as early as possible that new metrics will be introduced to measure, and therefore embed, the change you've asked for.

Why is this signal so hard to send?

Part of the problem is that reallocating resources and changing metrics aren't the glamorous work of strategic change. Rarely are mundane, instrumental, transactional leadership endeavors (such as resourcing or measurement) given much airtime in popular management literature or airport books. The result is that these more mundane aspects of leading change are still regarded as less important by leaders—although they remain some of the most critical signals for followers.

And, of course, making changes to resourcing and metrics takes time. The announcement of the strategic change might have missed the annual planning and budgeting round. While it's painful to face up to, announcing a major change might mean asking people to redo this grunt work. And while those asked to do it may not be immediately enamored with the request, they know the alternative is that they, and everyone else in the organization, will be second-guessing the change until this grunt work is done.

Now, it may take several months to define, agree, baseline, and then measure these new metrics, so start this work early (and just as importantly, talk about the fact that you're doing it). That way you signal to the organization what's coming and that the change is not a passing fad. Put your money where your mouth is, and send the signal that this change is your priority—and that it will be resourced and measured accordingly.

Signals Matter to Followers, So Signaling Needs to Matter to You

Followers are looking for signals to help them make sense of what they should do. As a leader, you have disproportionate power to shape these signals—or not. And that's especially important when you're asking for change. So supply people with what they need to make sense of it. And be the story you want their children to hear.

———————

Elsbeth Johnson, formerly a Professor at London Business School is now a senior lecturer at MIT's Sloan School of Management and the founder of SystemShift, a consulting firm.

NOTE

1. David A. Nadler and Michael L. Tushman, "Beyond the Charismatic Leader: Leadership and Organizational Change," *California Management Review* 32, no. 2 (1990): 77–97, https://doi.org/10.2307/41166606.

CHAPTER 12

Storytelling That Drives Bold Change

by Frances X. Frei and Anne Morriss

Let's say you're a leader with an urgent organizational problem—anything from a broken culture to a product that no longer fits your market. You've taken several steps toward a solution: You've identified the core issue and surfaced roadblocks to progress. You've run smart experiments that point the way forward. You've tapped the knowledge and earned the trust of everyone whose help you'll need, including people whose thinking is different from yours. With all that accomplished, you're

Reprinted from *Harvard Business Review*, November–December 2023 (product #R2306C).

ready to tackle a critical challenge: crafting a story so clear and compelling that it will harness your organization's energy and direct it toward change.

Research has shown that storytelling has a remarkable ability to connect people and inspire them to take action. "Our species thinks in metaphors and learns through stories," the anthropologist Mary Catherine Bateson has written. Tim O'Brien, who has won acclaim for his books about the Vietnam War, put it this way: "Storytelling is the essential human activity. The harder the situation, the more essential it is." When your organization needs to make a big change, stories will help you convey not only why it needs to transform but also what the future will look like in specific, vivid terms.

In this article, we outline an effective way to leverage the power of storytelling, drawing on decades of combined experience helping senior executives lead large-scale change initiatives. There are four key steps: Understand your story so well that you can describe it in simple terms; honor the past; articulate a mandate for change; and lay out a rigorous and optimistic path forward. Let's explore each of them in turn.

Understand Deeply, Describe Simply

This, we've observed in our work advising leaders, is the foundation of persuasive communication. If you understand something but can describe it only in complex or jargony language, you'll reach just the subset of people with expertise in the topic.

Consider T-Mobile's transformation from a company teetering on the edge of irrelevance to the serious player it is today. After he was named CEO in 2012, John Legere began listening in daily on customer service calls. As was widely reported in the press at the time, the experience led him to a fundamental truth about the wireless industry: People hated it. They resented being trapped in confusing contracts and hit with hidden fees. So he decided to offer clear service plans and transparent charges, among other innovations—in short, to become everything the industry wasn't. Legere understood the story of T-Mobile's change at such a profound level that he could communicate it in a single word: *uncarrier.*

When you think about the change you want to lead, ask yourself this: Can I capture my vision in a page? A paragraph? A word? The French philosopher Blaise Pascal once apologized for writing a long letter, explaining that he hadn't had time to write a short one. Your first task is to craft the equivalent of a short letter—even though it may take you extra time.

Honor Your Past

Your next step toward creating the future is to revisit the past, counterintuitive though that may seem. The process has two distinct stages.

Acknowledge the good parts of your history

It's easy to become so focused on the things you want to change that you forget to communicate what you *don't* want to. To get everyone on board with your ideas, you need to show that you truly understand the organization, starting with the good stuff.

There will always be self-appointed gatekeepers who are resistant to change—typically, valuable employees who have long institutional memories, care deeply about the organization, and worry about what might get lost in the transition. To bring them along, make it clear that you intend to preserve what's best about the company. Even the most logical change initiative can be unsettling and disruptive to those who'll be affected. Show people that you get it. We suggest having at least one gatekeeper stay close to you throughout the process so that you witness that person's concerns firsthand, which will make you more likely to respect and account for them.

In a study of large organizational change initiatives, the University of Amsterdam's Merlijn Venus and colleagues found that employees commonly feared their soon-to-be-transformed company would no longer be the organization they valued and identified with. The greater the uncertainty around the initiative, the greater the anxiety. Leaders were most effective in building support for change when they also emphasized continuity, the researchers found.

When Dara Khosrowshahi hosted his first town hall meeting as Uber's new CEO, in 2017, it might have been tempting to highlight the firm's missteps and position himself as its savior. Instead, he promised to "retain the edge that made Uber a force of nature," a remark met with thunderous applause. (Disclosure: One of us, Frances, is a former Uber employee.)

We were struck by Khosrowshahi's grace in that meeting. Follow his lead and show some sensitivity toward the people who aren't so sure about your plans for change: the skeptics, the resisters, and the simply scared. Honor the past they're holding on to, and they may gradually loosen their grip.

Reckon with the not-so-good parts

If your firm has lost the trust of any stakeholders, you'll need to rebuild it and earn the right to push forward. Spurred on by a courageous blog post by the software engineer Susan Fowler, in which she detailed her experience of harassment at Uber, Khosrowshahi combined his commitment to retain what was best about the company with a pledge to lead cultural change.

If your initiative is to capture employees' hearts and minds, you'll need to confront your organization's history with both optimism and honesty. Optimism means revealing your belief in a better tomorrow. Honesty means taking full responsibility for the things that went wrong and acknowledging the human costs of those mistakes.

For an example of taking clear, unequivocal responsibility for a painful past, we often point to the video game developer Riot Games (a company we've advised). In 2018 the organization issued a plainspoken apology on its website in response to public allegations of a fractured and sexist culture. "To all those we've let down . . . we're sorry," it began. "We're sorry that Riot hasn't always been—or wasn't—the place we promised you. And we're sorry it took so long for us to hear you."

Riot stands in stark contrast to many other companies that are called out for missteps. For instance, when the data engineer and whistleblower Frances Haugen publicly challenged Facebook (now Meta) to work harder to protect its most vulnerable users, the company's first response was to try to undermine her credibility. A tide of public frustration, a drop in the firm's stock price, and an increase in regulatory scrutiny followed. A good-faith attempt to engage with Haugen's rigorously documented charges would probably have yielded better results.

You don't need to have all the answers to begin addressing the difficult parts of your company's past. You do need to be willing to look at them unflinchingly and deal honorably with whatever you find. When Riot included with its apology a pledge to make the company "a place we can all be proud of," it didn't have all the details of its plan worked out. But it was definite about the fact that it needed one.

Provide a Clear and Compelling Mandate for Change

Now that you've honored the past—the good, the bad, and the ugly—and opened your stakeholders' minds at least somewhat to your message, it's time to share your rationale for creating a different future.

Begin by reflecting on the "why" of your plan. What problem are you trying to solve? What's the cost of not solving it? Your answers must be persuasive enough to override the comfort of familiar beliefs and behaviors. Among the challenges you may encounter is one put forward by Harvard Business School's Rosabeth Moss Kanter in Kanter's Law: *Everything looks like a failure in the middle.* You need to give people solid reasons to press on.

In 2010, faced with slumping sales and an anemic stock price, the new CEO of Domino's, Patrick Doyle, knew that to mount a successful turnaround he'd need to break through the malaise permeating the company culture. The chain was delivering handsomely on its promise to get customers pizza in record time. But as one reporter noted, "You then had to eat it." People had decided the pizza tasted so bad that in consumer tests, they rated the same pies lower when they knew they were from Domino's rather than a competing brand.

The conventional move would have been to quietly chip away at the problem while downplaying consumers' negative reactions. But Doyle and his team realized that a shock to the system was in order, so they decided to shine a bright light on customers' frustrations. They shared some of the scathing feedback in national ads and on a digital billboard in New York's Times Square. Comments like "worst excuse for pizza I've ever had" and "tastes like cardboard" scrolled in massive letters across its screen.

That bold move fueled fast, transformative change by making the need for it vividly clear. Stakeholders could not escape the fact that Domino's had a problem. Russell Weiner, the CMO at the time (he's now CEO), told *Inc.* magazine, "By saying what we said about the pizza, we blew up the bridge. That's what made it so much more powerful. If it didn't work out, there was no place to retreat to. There was no going back."

By leveling with consumers instead of trying to spin the situation, the company demonstrated its authenticity and engaged its market directly. Customers were given an essential truth-telling role in the campaign—and an excellent reason to pay attention to what happened next. After all, they'd been enlisted to co-create the needed fix—dubbed "Pizza Turnaround"—which hit the right deeply/simply notes.

What happened next was good for everyone. The chain's pizzas got a whole lot better, Pizza Turnaround grew same-store sales by more than 10% within a year, and the company's stock price took off.

Describe a Rigorous and Optimistic Way Forward

Your next step is to get into the weeds of your plan. What persuaded you to choose the road ahead? How confident are you that it's passable? In addressing those questions, you want to convey two things: rigor and, again, optimism. Data can help you demonstrate the first to stakeholders. Get comfortable with the numbers and pick just a few to use as plot points in your story. When it comes to data in storytelling, less is more.

When the Danish firm Ørsted set out to transform itself from an old-school power company into a leading provider of renewable energy, its management focused on a single ratio: 85%. The firm had historically generated that share of its energy from fossil fuels. In 2008 the leaders of the company (then called DONG Energy) decided to work toward flipping that ratio so that 85% would come from sustainable sources such as wind and solar. It labeled the initiative "85/15."

In communicating the plan, the company's leaders addressed hard truths about its strategic exposures, including climate change and the inevitable depletion of fossil fuel stores, with boldness and rigor. Henrik Poulsen, who was the CEO of Ørsted from 2012 to 2020, used that approach to enlist an initially skeptical workforce. "We set a long-term vision, then translate it into a strategic business ambition with tangible targets to guide it," he wrote in an online newspaper ad. "Then we roll that back into action items for each employee to focus on over the next year." Ørsted aimed to reach its goal in 30 years. It did so in a decade.

Now for the optimism part. Jeff Bezos famously asks his team to make the case for new ideas in structured six-page memos. Less famously, he asks people to pair those memos with hypothetical press releases, in part to test for the presence of genuine enthusiasm. In converting stakeholders to your vision, remember: Optimism is an infectious emotion that can be one of your most effective tools.

According to Gallup research, just 15% of U.S. employees "strongly agree" that their organization's leadership makes them enthusiastic about the future. To improve that number in your own organization, rigorously and optimistically describe your way forward.

Put the Pieces of Your Story Together

Now that you've taken those steps, it's time to combine the elements of your vision into a narrative and get others behind it. Ursula Burns, the CEO of Xerox from 2009 to 2016, who led the company through a major pivot from manufacturing to services, knows how effective that can be. Stories were the chief currency of her leadership. "One of the things I learned," she told the

2021 California Conference for Women, "was that stories matter, communications matter. Putting things in context matters." Burns spent countless hours meeting with stakeholders from around the world and making it clear that massive change was the only way forward—and that there was a better Xerox ahead. "Telling people the reality of what's going on and giving them hope by providing them with the vision . . . for what it's going to look like when we get through this is fundamental," she told attendees. "It's foundational to having people follow you."

Like Burns, you can assemble a change story that will inspire people to follow you. Use the structure we've discussed: Understand deeply and describe simply, honor the past, lay out the mandate for change, and provide a rigorous and optimistic vision for the future. Put your thoughts down on paper and, if practical, do it with your team. Share what you come up with to test and improve it. And remember that your customers are resources, too. Ask trusted ones for feedback—or take inspiration from Domino's and invite members of the public to add their voices to your story.

You needn't limit yourself to words (and the occasional number). When Jan Carlzon led the 1980s turnaround of Scandinavian Airlines (SAS), he circulated a small, illustrated pamphlet featuring a sad cartoon plane to convey the company's switch to a strategy anchored in delighting business travelers. As Carlzon detailed in his memoir, his fellow executives worried that SAS's cerebral Scandinavian workforce would reject the comic format and dismiss the message. But the pamphlet was widely embraced and helped the firm chart a course through turbulence and change. Carlzon's effort remains one of the most successful turnarounds in business history.

For a more recent example, consider Marguerite Zabar Mariscal, the CEO of the restaurant and retail brand Momofuku. She commissioned a beautifully designed pocket-size guidebook after the company reached 1,000 employees—too many for her to continue relying on intimate storytelling. Every new employee gets a copy of it.

Use words, numbers, cartoons, pictures—anything that helps activate your team—to bring your change story to life. Spark joy in the process, and stay open to the unexpected.

Repeat Yourself

Now tell your story wherever the opportunity arises: in speeches, interviews, town hall meetings, team huddles, one-on-ones. Push yourself outside your comfort zone and experiment with different formats. For example, high-quality videos are now easy for anyone with a smartphone to make, and they can be a powerful tool for showing—rather than simply telling—your story of change.

You'll probably need to communicate far more often than you think you should. In our experience, change leaders generally need to double or triple their pace of strategic messaging.

Why? Frequent communication ensures that busy, distracted stakeholders will internalize your story to the point where it reliably informs their actions. A core objective of change leadership is to set others up to succeed in your absence. That's essential to organizational speed because it means you won't become a bottleneck.

Alan Mulally talked incessantly about his "One Ford" turnaround plan when he was CEO of the car company. He started every meeting by reviewing it, and he had it distributed to every employee on a wallet-sized card. Bryce Hoffman, the author of a book on Mulally's time at Ford, wrote, "After six months, those of us who followed the company had gotten sick of hearing about [it]." When in one interview Hoffman asked Mulally if he'd be sharing something new, the CEO was incredulous. "We're still working on this plan," he replied. "Until we achieve these goals, why would we need another one?" That relentlessness paid off. In less than four years, Mulally pulled Ford back from the brink of bankruptcy and made it one of the most profitable automakers in the world.

Research by Harvard Business School's Tsedal Neeley and the University of California's Paul Leonardi validates Mulally's approach. After studying leaders in six companies for 250-plus hours and recording every communication, the pair discovered that leaders who were intentionally redundant moved their projects forward faster and more smoothly than others. "We're so bred to believe that clarity is the key to being a better communicator," Leonardi told HBR. "It's [actually] about making your presence felt. Employees are getting pulled in many directions and reporting to lots of people and getting tons of communications. So how do you keep your issues top of mind? Redundancy is a way to do that."

Dharmesh Shah, a cofounder of HubSpot, has written, "It took me 20-plus years as an entrepreneur to start to recognize the power of repetition—and even then it's still uncomfortable." (Disclosure: HubSpot is a client of the Leadership Consortium, an organization we started.) That sort of discomfort, Shah notes, signals that you're on the right track. "It's *natural* for it to feel *unnatural*," he continued. "Unnatural, but profoundly necessary." One test of whether you're communicating your change story often enough: Are you sick of hearing yourself talk? The answer should be yes.

Identify and Use Your Emotions

We'll close by talking about emotions—an underexplored part of leading change. Evolution has taught us to pay close attention to one another's feelings, particularly those of people with influence over our security and well-being. That unconscious vigilance can be both an asset and a liability for executives. It means that a leader's optimism is highly infectious—but so are emotions such as stress and anxiety.

Wanting to demonstrate the power of gratitude in the workplace, former PepsiCo CEO Indra Nooyi regularly sent thank-you notes to the *parents* of her senior team members, expressing appreciation for sharing their children with the firm. She wrote more than 400 notes a year. Some of Nooyi's colleagues—high-flying executives with résumés filled with accomplishments—told reporters it was the best thing that had ever happened to them.

Nooyi's notes embody what Daniel Goleman, the psychologist who developed the idea of emotional

10 UNDERRATED EMOTIONS IN CHANGE NARRATIVES

In addition to being powerful tools of persuasion, emotions can ground us and make us more authentic. Here are some that leaders tend to undervalue—in both storytelling for change and beyond.

- *Frustration.* The serial entrepreneur Paul English has tapped into this for every one of his breakthrough ideas. For example, he started the metasearch engine Kayak after spending vast amounts of time combing one airline website after another for flights.

- *Regret.* This typically relates to our interactions with others. We regret a careless comment or not saying something that could have made a difference. Uncomfortable as this emotion is, it often shows us what to do differently next time.

- *Enthusiasm.* The most effective change storytellers are evangelical about the future and reveal their excitement at every turn. Don't hold yourself back.

- *Devotion.* We sometimes withhold the full expression of our devotion—our commitment to someone else's success—in the mistaken belief that it will make it harder to hold that person accountable for performance. It won't.

- *Happiness.* The late Tony Hsieh built his shoe and clothing empire Zappos on a foundation of happy employees, customers, and suppliers. Let his legacy be that we listen more closely to the story he came to tell us.

- *Discomfort.* We are wired to avoid this feeling— yet so much good happens outside our comfort zone, whether it's learning something new or confronting an unfamiliar problem. As IBM's then-CEO Ginni Rometty told attendees at *Fortune*'s Most Powerful Women Summit, "Growth and comfort don't coexist."

- *Anger.* This is often a mask for more compli- cated feelings such as disappointment and sad- ness. When you're experiencing anger, do some emotional digging. What might be living beneath the anger? What can you learn from it? Can you harness it as a motivating force?

- *Joy.* This is one of NBA coach Steve Kerr's four core team values (along with mindfulness, com- passion, and competition), which Kerr credits with fueling the Golden State Warriors' success. That often surprises people—until they see the team cheerfully dominate the court.

(continued)

10 UNDERRATED EMOTIONS IN CHANGE NARRATIVES

- **Fellowship.** Life brings all of us to our knees at some point. We need other people to help us get back up, in big and small ways. That's just as true at work as anywhere else.

- **Grace.** This might take the form of kindness, compassion, or generosity of spirit. It might be a decision to have a difficult conversation—or not to. However it shows up, grace demands that we first practice it on ourselves in order to be credible conduits to others.

intelligence, would call *primal leadership*. He has described the phenomenon this way: "The leader's mood is quite literally contagious, spreading quickly and inexorably throughout the business. . . . The same holds true in the office, boardroom, or shop floor; group members inevitably 'catch' feelings from one another." When you're a leader, there's no button to turn off the broadcast feature on your feelings.

Many organizations experienced that reality in the early days of Covid-19. Researchers seeking communication lessons from the crisis surveyed some 800 employees. One finding was that the emotional note leaders hit could make or break an individual's commitment to the firm. "Our leader's reassurances . . . that the company has our backs are inspiring," one person said. "I even used

[them] . . . on social media to make sure people knew we are still hiring and that this is the sort of company you want to work for when the going gets tough."

Self-awareness is key to playing the instrument of your emotions and preventing them from sabotaging your change story. Accepting your feelings and integrating them into your actions also builds trust by reinforcing authenticity.

You may be familiar with this oft-cited statistic: Depending on the measurement used, up to 70% of organizational change efforts fail. But if you create a compelling narrative, you'll greatly increase your chances of defying those odds. Your story can transform your organization by shaping attitudes and beliefs, starting with your own. The story you tell yourself sets the stage for the organizational change you're envisioning. And when you share it skillfully with others, your story starts to become their reality.

———————

Frances X. Frei is the UPS Foundation Professor of Service Management at Harvard Business School and a coauthor of the books *Move Fast and Fix Things* and *Unleashed*.

Anne Morriss is an entrepreneur and the executive founder of the Leadership Consortium. She is also the coauthor of *Move Fast and Fix Things* and *Unleashed*.

CHAPTER 13

How to Raise a Difficult Issue with Your Boss

by Steven G. Rogelberg and Jon Gray

Gordon was stewing. He needed to share something with his manager about an ongoing conflict between himself and another team member, Ellen, but he was uncertain how to do it. Although he got along well with his boss, he was nervous about how she might respond. He committed to raising the issue at his next one-on-one meeting, but the meeting came and went and he failed to get up the courage to do it—and then he felt that bringing it up at a later date would be odd. Gordon was not only stewing,

Adapted from "How to Raise a Difficult Issue in a One-on-One with Your Boss," on hbr.org, January 9, 2024 (product #H07X0W).

he was pretty miserable and discontented, which took a toll on his engagement and productivity at work.

Likely all of us have been Gordon at times. (In fact, he's a composite of employees we've studied.) Wanting to raise a difficult or emotional issue to a manager is a common experience, whether it's about how to tell them that you're experiencing difficulties with a colleague; that your team is not going to hit a key deadline; that you're facing health issues; that you made a mistake; or that you have important feedback for them.

Here's the key to doing it well. In researching his new book *Glad We Met: The Art and Science of 1:1 Meetings*, one of us (Steven) surveyed and interviewed thousands of employees in a variety of organizations about what made for productive one-on-ones. He found that the most successful meetings are those in which the employee and manager are clear on and focused on the employee's needs. Here is a process for establishing your goals and keeping your conversation on target.

Step 1: Pick carefully

Overall, it is important to pick your battles wisely. To begin, consider the underlying key drivers of your concerns, rather than just their symptoms; what your manager can actually help with and what type of help might be needed; and priority items versus secondary items that can be discussed later. Also evaluate whether the issue might naturally resolve itself. Finally, consider factors such as the potential costs and benefits to sharing this information, and how your manager typically responds to feedback or difficult conversations.

For example, if Gordon's issue with his colleague Ellen is annoying but not affecting his work, and the project they're working on together is about to end, it may not be worth his raising the issue with his manager. But if it's causing delays in the project or threatens his future work with her, his manager needs to know.

Depending on your relationship, it might also help to let your manager know in advance that you're going to need their help resolving an issue or that you want to bring up something important or sensitive. This avoids blindsiding them and sets the stage for a constructive meeting.

Step 2: Ready yourself

Write down and practice your talking points in advance to get comfortable with them. Also consider how your manager might receive your comments. How will they react? What will they say? Envision and plan around their possible responses when practicing your talking points. This type of preparation can help you speak clearly and potentially allay nervousness at the time of the actual meeting. Research has shown that performance visualization can help reduce anxiety and improve your delivery.[1]

Step 3: Start well

Start the conversation off on the right foot to ensure that your comments are well received. Try to be upbeat, as mood states can be quite contagious.[2] Positive body language like smiling and soft eye contact can go a long way as well.

Confirm that your manager is willing to hear your feedback (e.g., "Is it still OK if I discuss . . .") and show gratitude for their willingness to do so (e.g., "Thank you for taking the time to hear about my concern. It really means a lot to me"). These expressions of gratitude are an example of showing deference through your speech, which researchers believe can influence how receptive your manager is to your requests for help.[3]

Step 4: Demonstrate composure, curiosity, and a willingness to adapt

When navigating the conversation, maintain your composure as best you can and share the core need you've identified sincerely and in an organized fashion. This is where you make it clear whether you're requesting your manager's help or you're just bringing something important to their attention. Continue to be mindful of your tone.

After sharing your feedback, listen attentively to your manager's response. Be curious and show your engagement by asking probing and clarifying questions. A great follow-up is simply: "Tell me more. Why do you suggest that?" This can give you clarity behind declarative answers from a boss. Acknowledge your manager's perspective, even if you might not agree with them. Negative emotions can cause breakdowns in communication, so try to remain positive and focused on working toward a common ground.

If you've presented an issue that needs to be resolved, come to the meeting with possible solutions already in mind. Research has shown that workers are viewed as more competent when they have potential solutions pre-pared at the time of communicating an issue with their manager.[4] Your proposed solutions don't have to be per-fect, but coming prepared with them is a signal of your proactivity and commitment to overcoming presented issues. Psychologists categorize help-seeking into two primary categories: autonomous and dependent.[5] De-pendent help-seeking involves looking for someone else to provide a "quick and easy" solution for you, whereas autonomous help-seeking refers to the pursuit of knowl-edge that empowers individuals to tackle challenges in-dependently and become self-sufficient. That's what you should aim for; research has shown that autonomous help-seeking behavior was related to positive job perfor-mance ratings, whereas dependent help-seeking was re-lated to negative ratings.[6]

If your manager suggests revisions to your proposed solution, be willing to adapt and make reasonable compromises. Patience and persistence throughout this process will lead you and your manager to a mutually de-sirable resolution.

Step 5: Wrap up while maintaining momentum

When ending the meeting, it's important to maintain the momentum you've built during your discussion. If you requested your manager's help during the meeting, verify action items that were assigned during the meet-ing and clarify both of your next steps. For example, as his meeting with his boss was coming to a close, Gor-don could summarize: "OK, so I'll talk to Ellen using the techniques we discussed, and you'll follow up with some other team members to see if additional issues are at play." And to end the meeting on a positive note, restate your gratitude for their time and receptiveness to your feedback.

Bringing up challenging topics with your manager involves careful planning and execution. Rest assured, the rewards are well worth the effort. The steps above will prepare you to navigate challenging communication with your manager and work toward desired outcomes. But they do more than that. They show you how to be an advocate for yourself—how you can sustain your independence and growth as you progress through your career.

———————

Steven G. Rogelberg is the Chancellor's Professor at the University of North Carolina Charlotte for distinguished national, international, and interdisciplinary contributions. He is the author of *Glad We Met: The Art and Science of 1:1 Meetings* and *The Surprising Science of Meetings: How You Can Lead Your Team to Peak Performance.* He writes and speaks about leadership, teams, meetings, and engagement. Follow him on LinkedIn or find more information at stevenrogelberg.com.

Jon Gray is an organizational science PhD student at the University of North Carolina Charlotte. He holds a master's degree in applied research and evaluation, and is a Certified Animal Welfare Administrator (CAWA). His research interests primarily focus on meeting science, as well as occupational stress faced by dirty work and caring professions. Follow him on LinkedIn.

NOTES

1. Joe Ayres and Tim Hopf, "Visualization: Reducing Speech Anxiety and Enhancing Performance," *Communication Reports* 5, no. 1 (1992): 1–10, DOI: 10.1080/08934219209367538.

2. Sigal G. Barsade, Constantinos G. V. Coutifaris, and Julianna Pillemer, "Emotional Contagion in Organizational Life," *Research in Organizational Behavior* 38 (2018): 137–151, https://doi.org/10.1016/j.riob.2018.11.005.

3. P. S. Rogers and S. M. Lee-Wong, "Reconceptualizing Politeness to Accommodate Dynamic Tensions in Subordinate-to-Superior Reporting," *Journal of Business and Technical Communication* 17, no. 4 (2003): 379–412, https://doi.org/10.1177/1050651903255401.

4. Jeffrey W. Kassing, "Speaking Up Competently: A Comparison of Perceived Competence in Upward Dissent Strategies," *Communication Research Reports* 22, no. 3 (2005): 227–234, DOI: 10.1080/00036810500230651.

5. Arie Nadler, "Personality and Help Seeking," in *Sourcebook of Social Support and Personality*, ed. Gregory R. Pierce, Brian Lakey, Irwin G Sarason, and Barbara R. Sarason (Boston: Springer, 1997), https://doi.org/10.1007/978-1-4899-1843-7_17.

6. Dvora Geller and Peter A. Bamberger, "The Impact of Help Seeking on Individual Task Performance: The Moderating Effect of Help Seekers' Logics of Action," *Journal of Applied Psychology* 97, no. 2 (2012): 487–497, https://doi.org/10.1037/a0026014.

Overcoming Roadblocks and Resistance to Change

CHAPTER 14

Overcome Resistance to Change with Two Conversations

by Sally Blount and Shana Carroll

Across industries and sectors, the track record for organizational change is bleak. Research finds that anywhere from 50% to 75% of change efforts fail.[1] And for those that do succeed, many don't achieve the goals of the original vision. Why is change so hard?

Usually, figuring out the right answer—whether it's a new strategy, more efficient processes or systems, or

Adapted from content posted on hbr.org, May 16, 2017 (product #H03NTA).

a new structure that better meets the needs of a growing company—is not the challenge. The biggest hurdle to effective organizational change is people. A core part of your job as a leader is to help others overcome the inherent, very human bias toward maintaining the status quo.

In our work leading change in higher education and teaching students and executives about the change management process, we've gained a deep understanding of why resistance happens and what leaders can do to overcome it.

Identifying the Sources of Resistance

You first need to identify who—that is, which individuals and groups—have the biggest potential to thwart positive change. Then you have to unstick them. Doing so begins with understanding their perspectives. In our experience, there are three primary reasons people resist.

Substance

Even if you've done your homework and have engaged a broad range of stakeholders in determining the new direction for your organization, team, or project, there are undoubtedly going to be people who disagree on substantive grounds. Maybe they don't agree with your analysis of the problem or they think they have unique experiences, expertise, or information that haven't been sufficiently considered. With this type of resistance, your job is to listen and be open to changing your approach based on what you learn.

Respect

A second universal source of resistance is the human need for respect, which frequently heightens during periods of change. This is especially true of employees who have been with an organization for a long time or have held a good deal of influence at some point in the past (and believe they still do). If these people don't feel that they've had a chance to weigh in, they will assume that an important perspective has been missed, that the answer can't be right if they have not been consulted. Again, the solution is to listen respectfully and make sure they feel heard.

Pace

Another reason people might resist is simply because they are feeling rushed. They don't have enough time to digest the new direction or cope with the situation emotionally. We all operate at different speeds. Here, your goal should be to figure out whether any timelines can be adjusted to reduce some of this time-based stress.

Talking with the Resisters

As you begin talking to resisters, keep in mind four ground rules.

Forget efficiency

Motivating true change requires unhurried, face-to-face, one-on-one conversation. Email doesn't do it, nor do instant messages, memos, or videos. If a specific work group or person is very important to your organization's future, and they are resisting needed change, you have to take the time to talk with them face-to-face and to do it under as little time pressure as possible.

Focus on listening

No matter how brilliant your plan or persuasive your argument, you must make everyone feel understood. That starts and ends with listening. When you're in these conversations, make sure to take up no more than 20% of the airtime, and when you do speak, be curious and try to repeat back what you've heard as much as possible.

Be open to change yourself

A resister who senses you are listening only so you can get what you want won't open up—and definitely won't get onboard. You must have an open attitude: Be ready to learn something new and, if necessary, modify your plans. Show that resisters' opinions and feelings matter to you and will shape your thinking and actions.

Have multiple conversations

We've found that effective dialogue with resisters typically requires a minimum of two conversations. In the first, you listen and diagnose the roots of the resistance. In the second, your goal is to make clear that you have reflected on what you heard, to outline what will be different—or not—in your approach to the change based on that conversation, and to explain why. Even if you're not changing your overall plan, we've found that anyone who truly listens to opposition will have their thinking changed in some way. So you can at least be genuine about that.

The time between these two conversations is critical. We recommend at least two days, depending on the scale of the change. If you respond immediately, either during the initial talk or within a few hours, resisters won't believe, perhaps rightly, that you've fully considered their point of view. But don't wait more than seven days, because at that point the person feels dismissed and forgotten.

Effective change management is critical to the vitality and progress of every organization. Where most people trip up is in failing to manage resistance effectively. Doing so requires an ability to listen to your opposition, diagnose their antipathy, consider their thoughts and feelings, and explain how it has changed your thinking, if not your plan. This is a time-consuming but effective process. As Jim McNerney, the former CEO of Boeing, said in one of our classes, "Change happens one conference room and one office at a time."

Sally Blount is the Michael L. Nemmers Professor of Strategy and the former dean at Northwestern University's Kellogg School of Management. She serves on the board of Abbott Laboratories.

Shana Carroll is Clinical Professor of Management and Organizations at the Kellogg School of Management at Northwestern University.

NOTE

1. "How to Beat the Transformation Odds," McKinsey & Company (2015), https://www.mckinsey.com/~/media/mckinsey/business%20functions/people%20and%20organizational%20performance/our%20insights/how%20to%20beat%20the%20transformation%20odds/how_to_beat_the_transformation_odds.pdf.

CHAPTER 15

What Are You Doing About Change Exhaustion?

by Mollie West Duffy and Liz Fosslien

Reorgs, leadership transitions, new technologies. Change affects every individual in every role in every industry. How can leaders help their teams combat change exhaustion—or step out of its clutches? Too often, organizations simply encourage their employees to be resilient, placing the burden of finding ways to feel better solely on individuals. Leaders need to recognize that

---

Adapted from "Managers, What Are You Doing About Change Exhaustion?," on hbr.org, May 4, 2022 (product #H07OYL).

change exhaustion is not an individual issue, but a collective one that needs to be addressed at the team or organization level.

Based on research we did for our book *Big Feelings*, here are four practices leaders can use to help their team or organization collectively combat change exhaustion.

Pause to acknowledge change, and the discomfort that comes with it

Navigating uncertainty requires that we push back against our natural impulse to run from discomfort. When faced with anxiety, we tend to immediately jump into action mode. Psychologists call this "anxious fixing," and it doesn't help us or the people around us.[1] Rather than addressing the root cause of our anxiety, we work ourselves into exhaustion trying to find immediate relief.

Say someone new is joining your team. As a leader, you may try to drum up excitement by sending a flurry of emails with brief bios and introductions and invitations for informal get-togethers without stopping to acknowledge the emotional toll the shift might take on your people. A study by Gartner found that smaller-scale, personal changes—getting assigned to a new manager or moving to a new team—were 2.5 times more fatiguing than larger transformational changes like mergers or acquisitions.[2] But how often do leaders pause when changing team assignments and give voice to the discomfort that employees may feel from these changes? We recommend having an employee's former manager meet with both the employee and the employee's new manager to talk through the details of the change, acknowledge the anxiety the employee may be feeling, and create space for the employee to share their emotions and ask questions.

Adopt the mantra, "I am a person who is learning _____."

Sitting with uncertainty helps us confront the fact that we don't have all the answers. Of course, that can be frightening, especially if you're someone who likes to feel in control. To help yourself and your team shift from anxiety to a growth mindset, reframe the situation. When we tell ourselves, "I am a person learning to _____" versus "I can't do this" or "I need to have this all figured out already," we start to see ourselves as empowered agents of change.

Here are a few examples of how you can reframe the not knowing:

- Instead of "I've never managed this many people before, I'm overwhelmed." Try, "I'm learning how to manage at a new scale, and I can always ask my mentors and peers for advice."

- Instead of "I'm a nervous wreck about the upcoming board meeting." Try, "I'm learning how to put together a compelling update and delegate tasks to clear up time for me to focus on the upcoming board meeting."

We recommend doing this as an exercise with your team by asking them to fill in the phrase, "I am a person learning to ____" or "We are a team learning to ____." It can be helpful to hear what others are navigating, so individual team members feel less alone and can more easily support each other. It can also be useful to better understand each person's comfort level with uncertainty.[3] If you know everyone on your team prefers to avoid uncertainty, for example, you can take extra steps to ensure that everyone understands the path forward.

Make a plan from which you will deviate

In the face of uncertainty, we have to work extra hard to figure out what we should do next. Our brains are hardwired to recognize patterns. When confronted with a known challenge (e.g., filling out a quarterly report), we can simply think, "Here's how I did this last time. I'll do that again."

Uncertainty breaks that mechanism. "You feel you have to pay closer attention to everything that's going on, because you're not confident about what you should do," psychologist Dr. Molly Sands told us. "That's why uncertainty is so exhausting."

That's also why it's easy to get stuck in analysis paralysis: Our minds are swamped as they zigzag through a million future possibilities. So how can you figure out a path forward under these circumstances?

At NASA, Dr. Laura Gallaher told us, teams refer to plans as "plans from which we deviate." Dr. Gallaher explained, "The benefit of planning is doing the thinking around what we will do when something happens. The value is in the process and the journey, not in the specific agenda." In other words, the key is to plan, but not see our plans as set in stone. Instead, view them as reassurance that we're prepared to face what comes next.

We recommend using similar language with your teams. By adopting a more flexible mindset while planning, you can help your people get less frustrated when things inevitably shift and be more willing to see the journey as a learning experience.

Invest in rituals

Studies show that rituals or habits can go a long way toward reducing our stress levels during times of uncertainty. Rituals provide structure and predictability, which give our brain a sense of control, thus lowering anxiety. It doesn't even matter what the ritual is, as long as it is well-practiced.[4]

It can be hard to stick to rituals as an individual within a larger organization. We've often added meditation or lunch breaks to our calendars, only to have another meeting scheduled over them or to find ourselves unable to tear ourselves away from our constantly pinging inboxes.

Organizational consultant Amy Bonsall, who helps organizations collectively achieve well-being, suggests teams ask, "How can we incorporate rituals as part of our days?" Bonsall says it doesn't matter what specifically teams do, as long as it is collective and centers on what matters most to that team (for example: energy boosting, creativity, or connection). She suggests starting each meeting with a short centering practice, like collectively closing your eyes and breathing for a minute. Or doing a daily 15-minute stand-up where everyone shares something that is inspiring them.

There is no doubt that uncertainty is anxiety-inducing. The key is to not let employees struggle alone, but to collectively acknowledge and address the challenges. With the right tools, you can help your team gain confidence in their ability to better handle whatever comes next together—whether that means establishing a "plan from which you'll deviate" or putting into practice a few new rituals (even if you don't believe in them).

———————

Mollie West Duffy is the coauthor of the *Wall Street Journal* bestseller *No Hard Feelings: The Secret Power of Embracing Emotion at Work* and *Big Feelings: How to Be Okay When Things Are Not Okay*. She is the head of Learning and Development at Lattice and was previously an Organizational Design Lead at global innovation firm IDEO and a research associate for the dean of Harvard Business School. She has worked with companies of all sizes on organizational development, leadership development, and workplace culture.

Liz Fosslien is the coauthor and illustrator of the *Wall Street Journal* bestseller *No Hard Feelings: The Secret Power of Embracing Emotion at Work* and *Big Feelings: How to Be Okay When Things Are Not Okay*. She is on the leadership team of Atlassian's Team Anywhere, where she helps distributed teams advance how they collaborate. Liz has designed and led workshops for executives at Google, Facebook, and Nike on how to create inclusive cultures. Her writing and work have been featured by TED, *The Economist, Good Morning America,* the *New York Times,* and NPR.

NOTES

1. Kathleen Smith, "Don't Try to Fix Anything Right Now," *Forge* on Medium, March 23, 2020, https://forge.medium.com/dont-try-to -fix-anything-right-now-eb28b99816e2.

2. "Gartner Survey Reveals HR Leaders' Number One Priority in 2022 Will Be Building Critical Skills and Competencies," press release, October 20, 2021, https://www.gartner.com/en/newsroom/press -releases/2021-10-20-gartner-survey-reveals-hr-leaders--number-one -priorit.

3. Liz + Mollie, "Take Our Uncertainty Tolerance Assessment on Your Own, and with Your Team," https://www.lizandmollie.com/ uncertainty-tolerance.

4. Elaina Hancock, "Life-Hack: Rituals Spell Anxiety Relief" UConn Today, June 30, 2020, https://today.uconn.edu/2020/06/ life-hack-rituals-spell-anxiety-relief/#.

CHAPTER 16

Keep Your Team Motivated When a Project Goes Off the Rails

by Rebecca Zucker

According to a report by TeamStage, 70% of projects globally fail.[1] And big projects and change initiatives, with greater complexity and more moving parts, fail at significant rates. This can be for a variety of reasons, ranging from passive project sponsors and inadequate resources to a shifting organizational context or lack of internal alignment and stakeholder buy-in.

Adapted from content posted on hbr.org, October 31, 2023 (product #H07VSV).

Poorly performing projects not only impact the bottom line, they also, understandably, impact morale and engagement. If your new initiative is going sideways or south, here are some ways to motivate your team to help get things back on track.

Reestablish or redefine the project purpose, goals, and vision

The project may not be going well because the organization's goals and vision aren't clear. In fact, a lack of clear goals is the most common factor in poor performance, leading to 37% of project failures.[2] A changing internal and external organizational context could affect the relevance of the project goals or stakeholder buy-in, as priorities shift. According to TeamStage, 44% of projects fail due to lack of alignment between the business and the project goals.

Getting the team together to reestablish or redefine these goals can breathe a second life into the project—assuming the context hasn't changed so much that the project is no longer relevant. No one likes working on the "road to nowhere." Research from the Standish Group shows that more than 30% of projects will get canceled prior to completion. According to Antonio Nieto-Rodriguez, author of *HBR's Project Management Handbook*, "Consider revising the project charter if necessary."

As part of this process, make sure you have executive sponsorship for the project. The TeamStage study also revealed that 62% of successfully completed projects had supportive sponsors. Nieto-Rodriguez observes that

"Having a high-level executive articulate the project's importance to the organization can give the team a renewed sense of purpose."

Involve the team in troubleshooting and defining the path forward

Enlist the team in troubleshooting in a collaborative way that doesn't place blame but seeks to get to the root cause and find a better path forward. Nieto-Rodriguez recommends holding a "state of the project" meeting where "everyone can express concerns and offer solutions without fear of retribution."

As the team leader, you can also create psychological safety and model a growth mindset by going first in sharing mistakes that you've made that might have contributed to the project's lackluster performance and what you've learned from them. In these meetings, encourage open communication and transparency, which not only builds trust, but also empowers the team to find a solution together. This reinforces a sense of "being in it together," which can bring a greater sense of motivation for the team.

Help remove obstacles

A key part of your job as leader is to help remove obstacles for the team. This includes reprioritizing or reassigning other work, and reallocating resources for the project—including people, time, and budget. According to research by the Standish Group, more than 50% of projects will cost almost double the original budget estimates.[3] "If possible, reallocate resources to alleviate bottlenecks," Nieto-Rodriguez suggests. "This may involve bringing in additional team members, extending timelines, or securing more budget."

Another obstacle you can eliminate as project leader is to provide role clarity for your team members. Role clarity can prevent the duplication of effort, working at cross-purposes, or the unnecessary friction on the team and morale issues that come with stepping on other people's toes.

Another one of these bottlenecks might be you. By empowering decision making among the project team members, not every decision needs to come to you. You can still give general guidance as to what's important to consider in these decisions, where you want to be kept informed, and what needs to be escalated to you.

Understand what motivates different team members

While some general principles will apply for everyone when it comes to motivating your project team, also recognize that different people are motivated by different things. Nieto-Rodriguez points out that "some are motivated by public recognition, others by monetary incentives, and still others by career development opportunities. Tailoring your approach can go a long way." Know what "currencies" are most important to each of your team members and what you have to offer to them individually. In addition to the ones mentioned above, these currencies can include visibility, gratitude or appreciation, support, creative freedom, or intellectual challenge, among others.

Connect regularly as a team

Scheduling a standing weekly project meeting can help create regular feedback loops about what's working and what's not working so course corrections can be made in a timely way, thereby keeping the project on track and increasing the chances of success. These regular check-ins will also allow the team to get important issues on the table for key discussions, debate, and decisions—while straightforward status updates can be done asynchronously on platforms like Slack.

These meetings can also provide the opportunity to do some team building in order to strengthen the relationships and connective tissue amongst team members, as well as ensure ongoing alignment. Nieto-Rodriguez explains, "Depending on the project's urgency, a short team-building session away from work can often reset the team's energy and improve collaboration."

Celebrate small wins and provide recognition

Recognizing small wins can help mark progress for the team and raise their spirits. Celebrating project milestones as a team can not only boost morale, but also give the team a sense of traction against their goals and feelings of optimism. Nieto-Rodriguez points out that achieving even minor milestones can be a source of motivation.

In addition, providing individual recognition that is personalized can also help motivate team members, keeping in mind that introverts tend to prefer more private, one-on-one recognition and extroverts tend to appreciate more public recognition.

By focusing on the above strategies, you can both reenergize your project team and help put a poorly performing project back on track, creating a virtuous cycle that leads to the project and team's success.

———————

Rebecca Zucker is an executive coach and a founding partner at Next Step Partners, a leadership development firm. Her clients have included Amazon, Clorox, Morrison Foerster, Norwest Venture Partners, The James Irvine Foundation, and high-growth technology companies like DocuSign and Dropbox. Follow her on social media at @rszucker

NOTES

1. "Project Management Statistics: Trends and Common Mistakes in 2023," TeamStage, https://teamstage.io/project-management-statistics/#:~:text=What%20percentage%20of%20projects%20fail,shifting%20project%20objectives%2C%20and%20more.

2. "Project Management Statistics: Trends and Common Mistakes in 2023."

3. Anthony Mersino, "Project Managers Fail to Help Software Projects (Standish Group Chaos 2020)," Vitality Chicago, November 22, 2023, https://vitalitychicago.com/blog/project-managers-fail-to-help-software-projects-standish-group-chaos-2020/.

CHAPTER 17

How to Handle the Pessimist on Your Team

by Amy Gallo

Dealing with a pessimist on your team can be a frustrating and time-consuming experience, especially during a change transformation. Attempts to ignore or counter frequent negative comments may simply incite further negativity. Good news: By being proactive, you can help the pessimist change his behavior and enable your team to achieve greater productivity.

Adapted from content posted on hbr.org, September 17, 2009 (product #H003TJ).

What the Experts Say

The first step is to figure out what is causing your team member's negativity. Roderick Kramer, William R. Kimball Professor of Organizational Behavior at Stanford Graduate School of Business, says that it is the role of the leader to understand the underlying cause of the pessimism before acting. "Some people are dispositional pessimists whose knee-jerk reaction is to see the negative in everything, while others may be expressing a pessimistic point of view based on informed logic," Kramer says. Some common sources of pessimism include resentment at not having been promoted, a need for attention, or a need to cover for a lack of knowledge or skill.

Whatever the source of the pessimism, the key to responding constructively is to focus on the impact of the individual's behavior, according to Marshall Goldsmith, executive educator and the author of *What Got You Here Won't Get You There*. Changing behavior is much easier than trying to reform a person's long-held beliefs and values.

Here are three approaches to managing negative behavior:

Create awareness

This is best done by pulling the team member aside and explaining how their comments are received. The rule when giving this type of feedback, says Jon Katzenbach, author of *Wisdom of Teams* and founder of the Katzenbach Center at Strategy&, is to "be at least as positive as you are negative." Explain why the person is valued on the team and make clear the impact of their behavior. For example, you can say, "When you make negative comments, the team gets stuck and we aren't able to move forward." Kramer points out, "This kind of conversation can be useful from a diagnostic perspective." Once you understand the underlying reason for the pessimism, you can provide additional support or information if it's needed.

Reposition negative statements

Negativity can fester and eventually kill a team's momentum and motivation. Don't let negative comments linger. Ask for clarification or more information about what the speaker means. For example, if a team member says, "This project is never going to make it past Finance," ask the speaker to explain why they think that. Better yet, ask for alternative solutions: "What can we do to make sure the project *does* make it past Finance?" You can also ask team members to use "'but' statements." Ask them to follow skeptical or critical sentences with "but." For example, your team member could say "This project is never going to make it past Finance, *but* it's worth laying the groundwork now because next year, Finance is apt to approve more tech projects." It's helpful to model this type of behavior for the entire team. Offer your own constructive criticism while providing an alternative solution.

Involve the whole team

It can be damaging to single out a team member in front of the entire team. Peer pressure is a far more effective tactic. According to Kramer, "Sometimes social sanctions work better than leader sanctions." Set team norms and ask everyone to observe them. Goldsmith suggests that individuals ask themselves before they speak, "Will this comment help our customers? Will this help our company? Will this help the person or team we're talking about? Will this help the person we're talking to?" As he points out, "Honesty may be the best policy except when it's destructive and unhelpful." Once you've agreed on norms, ask the team to hold each other to them. This approach can be used when you're not the team leader as well. If a fellow team member is regularly negative, appeal to what Kramer calls "the collective wisdom" of the team by modeling positive behavior and using peer pressure to show the pessimist a more productive way of contributing. Of course, as a peer, your influence is limited, and you may need to talk with the team leader if your attempts to redirect the pessimist don't work.

When All Else Fails

All the experts agree that if a team member is continually disruptive and does not respond to coaching or feedback, you may ultimately need to remove them from the team. Sometimes people are not a good fit for a team or a project, and it's your job as leader to make that distinction.

Negativity Can Be Useful

It's important to remember that the goal here is not to rid the team of any skeptical sentiment. Not all negativity is bad, despite how it sounds or feels. According to Kramer, habitual pessimists' concerns may in some cases be well informed and rational and "based on an intuition or insight that could be extremely helpful to the group." For example, there were pessimists at NASA who didn't feel the Space Shuttle *Columbia* was ready to launch, especially after the *Challenger* disaster seven years earlier. We need dissenting voices to check our assumptions and push our ideas. Katzenbach says, "An irritating member adds a dimension to teaming. As long as they are not strong enough to derail progress, they may offer thoughts that otherwise wouldn't come in."

Case Study: Turning Negative Comments into Constructive Ones

Lisa Schneider, a sales director at an online media company, was leading a team to organize the company's sales inventory and identify operational efficiencies in the way they leveraged the inventory in new sales. Many of the team members were not Lisa's direct reports but people from other departments. Fred worked for Operations and from the beginning of the team's work together was skeptical of the project. He said over and over, "This isn't going to work." Lisa could see that Fred's attitude was having an effect on the other team members and was concerned he would ultimately impede the team's progress. She pulled Fred aside and explained that whenever he made negative comments, the team looked deflated and the conversation stopped. Fred was receptive to what she had to say, but he believed that Operations would not be able to execute on the ideas they were putting forth. Lisa told Fred that his boss, the head of Operations, believed in this project and had asked him to join the team for a reason. She asked him to offer alternatives to the ideas being proposed in addition to raising concerns. "I explained to Fred that what he was doing felt like continually putting up roadblocks without providing a detour sign. I asked that he propose additional solutions to overcome the obstacles he was raising," Lisa said. He took Lisa's advice to heart and began engaging with the team on new solutions. Team members were relieved to see Fred contributing in a positive way and openly debated the merits of the solutions he proposed.

Ultimately, the team's recommendations were implemented with many of Fred's alternative solutions incorporated. Lisa believes the end results were more rigorous because of Fred's contributions. The project was considered a success, and the new system has saved Operations 100 hours of work each quarter.

Case Study: Pessimism as Cover

Rutger von Post, a principal at Strategy&, led a team with a difficult team member. Joe was a junior consultant reporting to Rutger on this particular client project. Joe continually expressed skepticism about how the team was sizing the market for a new health-care product. The team met several times to go over the project, clearly divide up the work, and set goals and milestones. Joe did not productively contribute to any of these discussions. In fact, he would cross his arms and say things such as, "I don't see how this is useful for the client." Rutger pulled him aside in an attempt to understand what was causing Joe's negativity. Only after Rutger gave him direct and stark feedback about his behavior and the impact on his performance did

Joe make clear that he was acting skeptical because he didn't know how to do what was asked of him. Rutger spent a half day with Joe going over what he needed to do and practicing the work with him. Together, they sized 5 of 30 subsegments of the market so Joe would then be comfortable doing the rest of the work on his own. Rutger said, "Once he was shown how to do it, his skepticism evaporated." Joe eventually became a productive member of the team once Rutger understood and addressed the real source of his pessimism.

Amy Gallo is a contributing editor at *Harvard Business Review*, cohost of the *Women at Work* podcast, and the author of two books: *Getting Along: How to Work with Anyone (Even Difficult People)* and the *HBR Guide to Dealing with Conflict*. She writes and speaks about workplace dynamics. Watch her TEDx talk on conflict and follow her on LinkedIn.

Building Your Team's Agility for the Long Term

CHAPTER 18

How to Embrace Change Using Emotional Intelligence

by Kandi Wiens and Darin Rowell

Have you ever reacted to organizational change by rolling your eyes and quietly saying to yourself, "Here we go again"? Or by not-so-quietly asking others, "Haven't we tried this before?"

Changes at work can be emotionally intense, sparking confusion, fear, anxiety, frustration, and helplessness. Experts have even said that the experience of going

---

Adapted from content posted on hbr.org, December 31, 2018 (product #H04PW8).

through change at work can mimic that of people who are suffering from grief over the loss of a loved one.[1] Because change can be so physically and emotionally draining, it often leads to burnout and puts into motion an insidious cycle that leads to even greater resistance.[2]

No one wants to be an obstacle to change, instinctively resisting any new initiatives or efforts. It's not good for you, your career, or your organization. Improving your adaptability, a critical emotional intelligence competency, is key to breaking this cycle. Fortunately, this is a skill that can be learned. In fact, in our work as coaches, it's often a priority for our clients. They're tired of feeling frustrated and angry about changes at work, and they want to be seen as adaptable rather than resistant.

Next time your organization introduces a big change, consider these four emotional intelligence strategies to help you *embrace* the change rather than *brace for* it:

Identify the source of your resistance

Understanding the underlying reasons for your resistance requires a high level of self-awareness. For example, if you're resisting because you're worried that the change will make you look incompetent, you can create a learning plan for the new skills you will need in order to be successful. Or, if you're concerned that the change will interfere with your autonomy, you can ask the people leading the effort how you can be involved in the process. Even if you don't like the direction the organization is moving, being involved in the implementation may help you regain a sense of control and reduce your urge to resist.

Question the basis of your emotional response

Our emotional reactions to change often reflect our interpretations—or "stories"—that we convince ourselves are true. In actuality, our stories are often subconscious and seldom in line with reality. Ask yourself: *"What is my primary emotion associated with this change?" "Is it fear, anger, frustration?"* Once you identify the emotion, ask "What that's about?" *"What do I believe to be true that's making me angry/fearful/frustrated?"* This type of questioning helps to illuminate the stories driving our emotions and influence our perceptions.

As an example, a senior executive in the transportation industry identified her intense emotional reaction as anger. As she continued to question the basis of her anger, she discovered an underlying story: She was powerless and a victim of the impending change initiative. With this new awareness she was able to separate her emotional reaction and "story" from the actual events. This allowed her to identify several options to take on new leadership responsibilities for a major aspect of the change initiative. With these new opportunities to take back her power, her mentality shifted from thinking that the changes were happening to her to focusing on how she could take on a leadership role that would create new opportunities for both her career and the organization.

Own your part in the situation

It's not always easy to admit to the part we play in creating a negative situation. A self-aware person reflects on how their attitudes and behaviors contribute to their experience of the change. For example, let's say that you've noticed yourself becoming increasingly and more immediately tense each time you hear of a new change. Practicing mindfulness will allow you to examine your feelings and how they are affecting your attitude. Any negativity or pessimism is going to impact your behavior, performance, and well-being (and not in a good way). By reflecting on how your initial reaction contributes to a negative chain of events, it'll be easier to adjust your attitude to be more open to considering new perspectives, which will ultimately change the way you react to everything.

Turn up your positive outlook

Things may feel a little bleak when you don't agree with a new change, but studies show that having a positive outlook can open us up to new possibilities and be more receptive to change.[3] Asking yourself a few simple questions will help you think more optimistically. First, ask yourself *"Where are the opportunities with this change?"* And then, *"How will these opportunities help me and others?"*

For example, one of our clients recently went through a major organizational change. Over the previous 18 months, he had led the turnaround and sale of a division for his former company and had just accepted a new role as president with a new firm. He knew this wasn't something he would've been able to do a few years earlier. But he had worked hard to move from being a "problem solver" to an "opportunity finder." He explained how our work together prepared him: "I was always playing defense, focusing on how to minimize our exposure or losses in any situation. As we began to shift my focus from how to minimize losses to find opportunities, everything changed. I shifted from playing defense to offense. I began to see opportunities that were invisible to me before. Now, it's hardwired into how I think."

The ability to quickly and easily adapt to change is often a competitive advantage for a leader. Next time you feel yourself resisting, use these four approaches above to build momentum and psychological energy for you and others. Make the intentional choice not just to embrace change but to positively propel it forward.

––––––––

Kandi Wiens is a senior fellow at the University of Pennsylvania Graduate School of Education and the author of the forthcoming book *Burnout Immunity: How Emotional Intelligence Can Help You Build Resilience and Heal Your Relationship with Work*. A nationally known researcher and speaker on burnout, emotional intelligence, and resilience, she developed the Burnout Quiz to help people understand if they're at risk of burning out: kandiwiens.com/burnout-quiz/.

Darin Rowell is a senior adviser and executive coach who helps individuals and teams thrive in high-demand environments. His clients range from CEOs of high-growth companies to Division I head coaches. In addition to his advisory work, Darin is an active researcher in the area of executive performance and resilience.

NOTES

1. Jane Henderson-Loney, "Tuckman and Tears: Developing Teams During Profound Organizational Change," *SuperVision* 57, no. 5 (May 1996), https://www.avannistelrooij.nl/wp/wp-content/uploads/2014/08/Henderson-Loney-1996-Tuckman-Tears-Super.pdf; "The Five Stages of Grief: An Examination of the Kübler-Ross Model," Psycom, updated June 7, 2022, https://www.psycom.net/stages-of-grief.

2. Carl-Ardy Dubois, et al. "Why Some Employees Adopt or Resist Reorganization of Work Practices in Health Care: Associations between Perceived Loss of Resources, Burnout, and Attitudes to Change," *International Journal of Environmental Research and Public Health* 11, no. 1 (2014): 187–201, https://doi.org/10.3390/ijerph110100187.

3. Quy Nguyen Huy, "Emotional Capability, Emotional Intelligence, and Radical Change," *Academy of Management Review* 24, no. 2 (1999): 325–45, https://doi.org/10.2307/259085.

CHAPTER 19

Increase Your Return on Failure

by Julian Birkinshaw and Martine Haas

One of the most important—and most deeply entrenched—reasons why established companies struggle to grow is fear of failure. Indeed, in a 2015 Boston Consulting Group survey, 31% of respondents identified a risk-averse culture as a key obstacle to innovation.

Senior executives are highly aware of this problem. On one hand, they recognize the usefulness of failure. As 3M's legendary chairman William McKnight once said, "The best and hardest work is done in the spirit of adventure and challenge. . . . Mistakes will be made." Pixar's president, Ed Catmull, has a similar point of view. "Mistakes aren't a necessary evil," he has said. "They aren't

---

Reprinted from *Harvard Business Review*, May 2016 (product #R1605G).

evil at all. They are an inevitable consequence of doing something new . . . and should be seen as valuable."

On the other hand, management processes for budgeting, resource allocation, and risk control are built on predictability and efficiency, and executives get promoted by showing they're in control. So even if people understand that they can and *should* fail, they do everything possible to avoid it.

But there's a way to resolve this conundrum: Rigorously extract value from failure, so you can measure—and improve—your return on it, boosting benefits while controlling costs.

In a return-on-failure ratio, the denominator is the resources you've invested in the activity. One way to raise your return is by reducing this number—by keeping your investments low. Or you can deliberately sequence them, starting with small amounts, until major uncertainties have been resolved. The numerator is the "assets" you gain from the experience, including information you gather about customers and markets, yourself and your team, and your operations. Increasing these is the other way to boost your return.

In the 10-plus years we've spent researching team and organizational dynamics and working with more than 50 companies across a dozen industries, we've found that when people adopt the right mindset, they can increase this ratio—not just by minimizing the downsides of projects but also by maximizing the upsides. Some failures provide immediate value in the form of market insights that can be capitalized on. Others provide broader lessons that lead to significant personal or organizational development.

There are three steps you can take to raise your organization's return: First, study individual projects that did not pan out and gather as many insights as possible from them. Second, crystallize those insights and spread them across the organization. Third, do a corporate-level survey to make sure that your overall approach to failure is yielding all the benefits it should.

Step 1: Learn from Every Failure

Begin by getting people to reflect on projects or initiatives that disappointed. Of course, this doesn't come naturally: Reviewing past problems isn't just tedious; it's painful. Most of us would prefer to invest our time looking forward, not back. To help people answer the right questions, we've developed an exercise that categorizes all the sources of value that might accrue from a failed project and all the costs. Though we've just begun to test it in organizations, so far it's yielding promising results.

When something doesn't go as planned, it's an opportunity to challenge your default beliefs and adjust accordingly. We recommend spelling out what the project has taught you about each of these things: customers and market dynamics; your organization's strategy, culture, and processes; yourself and your team; and future trends. These insights, of course, are the assets. Our exercise also has you compile a list of the associated liabilities—the project's direct costs in time and money, any external costs (reputation, for example), and any internal indirect costs (such as excessive consumption of management attention).

Consider how this approach played out at a daily newspaper in the United Kingdom. A few years ago, the

ASSESSING A PROJECT'S RETURN ON FAILURE

Use our Project Review Worksheet to get a complete picture of the benefits and costs of your failed project.

TABLE 19-1

The Project Review Worksheet

Even when initiatives flop, they can still provide tremendous value to your organization—if you examine them carefully and capture the critical lessons. This template will help you do that.

Briefly describe a recent failed project or activity you were involved in:

Now answer the following questions:

ASSETS	LIABILITIES
1. What have we learned about our customers' needs and preferences and our current markets? Should we change any of our assumptions?	1. What were the direct costs—for materials, labor, and production?
2. What insights have we gained into future trends? How should we adjust our forecasts?	2. What were the external costs? Did we hurt our reputation in the market or with customers, or weaken our competitive position?

ASSETS	LIABILITIES
3. What have we discovered about the way we work together? How effective are our organizational processes, structure, and culture?	3. What were the internal costs? Did the project damage team morale or consume too much attention? Was there any organizational fallout?
4. How did we grow our skills individually and as a team? Did the project increase trust and goodwill? Were any developmental needs highlighted?	

Key insights and takeaways for the business:

CEO asked one of his brightest young editors to work with colleagues from marketing, design, and technology to prototype a new tabloid format and test it with customers. The experiment led to two important realizations: First, despite what people said in market research studies, they preferred traditional broadsheets or digital alternatives. Second, the small cross-functional team was a highly effective way to develop new editorial products. But perhaps the biggest lesson was a personal one. Because the young editor in charge of the project felt he had failed, he took a job elsewhere. Though the CEO might have chalked this up only in the liability category, he turned it into an asset by recognizing where he had made a critical misstep and growing from it. The young editor "thought he was developing a pilot, where success is about making it work," the CEO told us. "But for me it was an experiment, where success is about confirming or refuting a hypothesis. I should have been much more explicit with him." The CEO publicly took full blame for the departure and committed to communicating more clearly and encouraging a culture of experimentation going forward.

A second example comes from an elite consulting firm that lost a juicy new government contract to a much less prestigious competitor. This was a big and unexpected blow. But through a painstaking review, including an hourlong discussion in an executive committee meeting, the team members involved increased their return on this failure. They realized that the government's selection criteria were subtly different from what they had expected and that their competitor had been far more savvy in understanding what was needed and working with officials to position its bid. As the discussion progressed, deeper insights began to surface. The team had misjudged the criteria because they'd been complacent, making assumptions instead of investing time in finding out what the government wanted. And the firm hadn't even put its best people on the job, assuming its brand would be enough. "The truth is, we didn't take the whole process nearly as seriously as our competitor did, and we got burned," one executive commented. In other words, the real value of the failure was learning that the firm needed to dramatically change how it responded to opportunities.

We've found that when you encourage people to talk about projects in this way, the resulting conversation is illuminating. It forces them to think about everything they've learned, how that might help them move forward, and all the positive side effects gleaned from the experience.

Step 2: Share the Lessons

While it's useful to reflect on individual failures, the real payoff comes when you spread the lessons across the organization. As one executive commented, "You need to build a review cycle where this is fed into a broader conversation." When the information, ideas, and opportunities for improvement gained from an unsuccessful project in one business area are passed on to another, their benefits are magnified.

Shared learning also increases the likelihood of future initiatives. "The biggest mistake you can make as a

EXPERIMENTING WITH FAILURE
REVIEWS AT ROCHE

Pharmaceutical companies operate in a high-stakes environment where the rewards for successful innovation are huge, but the vast majority of drug discovery projects fail. As a leading player in the industry, Roche is always on the lookout for ways of working that will help it get the right balance between risk taking and caution.

To capture the benefits of experimentation, a cross-business team at Roche launched an initiative in 2015 implementing individual project-failure reviews. They identified 10 teams (of six to 15 people) working in different parts of the company and asked the leader of each to conduct a three-month pilot.

In kickoff meetings, groups were reminded of the importance of learning from failure and then asked to discuss a recent failed project. At two to four more follow-up meetings, team members were encouraged to share more examples of their own failures.

Participants embraced the process tentatively. As one team leader explained, "In the first meeting some people were very guarded, but the second worked much better and went on longer than planned." But another leader said that as the pilot progressed, he was "surprised by how candid people were with each other."

The reviews helped many participants recognize the personal growth they'd derived from failures. One manager described a project that had been derailed because she pushed it too far along without buy-in from other internal stakeholders. Another talked about being so focused on hitting his numbers in a new leadership role that he failed to pick up on problems that members of his team were having. Both learned from those incidents and changed their tactics accordingly.

Other participants noted new insights about their customers or markets. One team realized it had lost a major sale because it was so focused on its own agenda that it wasn't listening to or addressing its customer's questions. In another case, the failure happened because a team hadn't discerned who the real decision maker in the client organization was. Their main contact appeared to be in charge of the bid and gave them information, but he was not that influential. Those discussions helped Roche improve how it managed key relationships.

Another general benefit was team building. "It was a great opportunity to help my newly formed team work more collectively," said one leader. Another agreed: "The process helped us diffuse some tensions in the group."

Suggestions for improvement to the process also surfaced. For instance, one team leader suggested steering the discussion toward specific and recent projects to ensure that the recommendations generated were immediately relevant. "Some people protected themselves a bit, talking about things that

(continued)

EXPERIMENTING WITH FAILURE REVIEWS AT ROCHE

happened a couple of years ago, which is fine if you want to improve the team's sharing culture, but the market-based insights are more limited," she noted.

But all the team leaders agreed that structured, semiformal failure reviews were useful. As one put it, "It doesn't come naturally to share failures, and you have to give people time, so you cannot really do this as part of the regular rhythm of meetings. You need to create the space for it to happen, to put it on the calendar."

---

leader is to shoot the messenger and bury the bad news," one executive noted. By reflecting on the positives, you build trust and goodwill and clear the pathway for others to take action on riskier ideas.

We recommend bringing senior leaders (across a unit or the whole organization) together on a regular basis to talk about their respective failures. These reviews work best when they are *fast* and to the point; take place *frequently*, through good times and bad; and are *forward-looking*, with an emphasis on learning. We call them Triple F reviews.

When Kal Patel was brought in as head of Best Buy's Asian operations in 2009, he implemented this approach. The company had acquired a Chinese retail chain, Five Star, a few years earlier, and it was performing well. But the Best Buy branded stores were struggling. Patel pushed the store managers to make a lot of changes—new layouts, ways of working with suppliers, and pricing models—and instituted weekly unit meetings. "On Friday mornings, we'd have a review: 'What did you set out to learn?' 'What did you learn?' 'What is it costing you?' Bang, five to 10 minutes, move on to the next team." Ultimately, he recommended closing down all the Best Buys in China. But because he was also overseeing the Five Star chain, he was able to transfer a lot of the insights gleaned to that operation and retain most employees, and he also conveyed what he'd learned to other members of the leadership team.

Another example comes from a dairy food manufacturer. A review of a failed technology project revealed that although problems had surfaced two months in, it took the investment committee four more months to pull the plug. When the team leader pointed this out to his colleagues and bosses, there was momentum for a faster-cycle review process to ensure that failing projects would be killed more quickly in the future.

We have even seen some organizations create formal structures for sharing lessons from failures with all employees. At Engineers Without Borders International, a not-for-profit that strives to improve the quality of life in disadvantaged communities worldwide, executives were so frustrated with the limited knowledge transfer among their various affiliates that they launched an annual "failure report" that publicized, for all to see, the projects that were the biggest flops.

Informal approaches work too, however. The key is to capture relevant lessons with sayings or stories that catch on beyond the project's immediate circle and eventually become corporate folklore. At the U.K. newspaper, the CEO's distinction between pilot and experiment was repeated around the company. At the elite consulting firm, the tale of the lost bid became a shorthand way to remind colleagues to check their arrogance. At Coca-Cola, stories about the failure of New Coke are still told 30 years on.

Step 3: Review Your Pattern of Failure

The third step is to take a bird's-eye view of the organization and ask whether your overall approach to failure is working. Are you learning from every unsuccessful endeavor? Are you sharing those lessons across the organization? And are they helping you improve your strategy and execution?

Venture capital firms are very disciplined about examining their review process in this way. At Hoxton Ventures, for instance, partners sit down for half a day every quarter and go over the businesses they've invested in, asking if they've gotten something fundamentally wrong and looking for patterns. "It's easy to be swayed by one big success or failure," says partner Hussein Kanji, "so we push ourselves to do this systematically." At the 2008 Future of Management conference, Silicon Valley investor Steve Jurvetson observed, "You have to strive for a process of decision making that over a large number of decisions gives good outcomes. It's not 'Are we making good decisions?' but 'Do we have a process for making decisions that is statistically working?'"

These discussions should help you determine whether your failure rate is too high, too low, or just right. Sometimes you'll find you need to tighten up your systems. Consider a mining company we worked closely with. In the early 2000s, it was obsessive about its post-investment review process. Projects that did not yield a positive return were analyzed carefully and then analyzed again. But during the resource industry boom of the mid-2000s, the company got overconfident, and enthusiasm for these reviews faded. They still happened, but inconsistently. The company subsequently made two spectacularly bad acquisitions, leading to a massive write-down and a change in leadership. The new CEO, unsurprisingly, came in with a "back to basics" mandate, including a return to the old post-investment review process.

In other cases, a corporate-level review will show that you need to nudge your people toward greater openness to failure. We've seen several firms create awards celebrating failure: New York ad agency Grey has a Heroic Failure award; NASA has a Lean Forward, Fail Smart award; and the Tata Group has a Dare to Try award, which had 240 submissions in 2013. "We want people to be bold and to not be afraid to fail," Sunil Sinha, the head of Tata Quality Management Services, told *Bloomberg Businessweek* in 2009.

Failure is less painful when you extract the maximum value from it. If you learn from each mistake, large and small, share those lessons, and periodically check that these processes are helping your organization move more efficiently in the right direction, your return on failure will skyrocket.

———————

Julian Birkinshaw is a professor at London Business School. He is the coauthor of *Fast/Forward: Make Your Company Fit for the Future.*

Martine Haas is the Lauder Chair Professor of Management at the Wharton School and Director of the Lauder Institute for Management & International Studies at the University of Pennsylvania. Her research focuses on collaboration and teamwork in global organizations.

CHAPTER 20

How to Overcome Your Fear of the Unknown

by Nathan Furr and Susannah Harmon Furr

Humans are wired to fear the unknown. That's why uncertainty—whether at the macro level of a global economic, health, or geopolitical crisis or at the micro level
(Will I get that job? Will this venture be successful? Am
I on the right career path?)—can feel nerve-racking, exhausting, and even debilitating. However, that gut reaction leads people to miss a crucial fact: Uncertainty and
possibility are two sides of the same coin.

Reprinted from *Harvard Business Review*, July–August 2022 (product
#R2204L).

Consider the achievements you're most proud of, the moments that transformed your life, the relationships that make your life worth living. We'll bet that they all happened after a period of uncertainty—one that probably felt stressful but that you nevertheless pushed through to accomplish something great. When we moved abroad, for example, we faced uncertainty about making less money, paying higher taxes, doing more-challenging work, and introducing our children to new schools, a new language, and a new culture. But seven years later, we are so grateful for all the possibilities the move opened up.

Our modern-day heroes all have a similar story. Rosa Parks faced great uncertainty when she refused to give up her seat, igniting the Montgomery bus boycott and paving the way for desegregation. Nearly everyone initially thought that Elon Musk and his team would fail when they set out to revolutionize electric vehicles and push the world toward a more environmentally friendly future. They couldn't have achieved their breakthroughs if they had been afraid of uncertainty.

Uncertainty doesn't have to paralyze any of us. Over the past decade, we have studied innovators and changemakers who've learned to navigate it well, and we've reviewed the research on topics like resilience and tolerance for ambiguity. The findings are clear: We all can become adept at managing uncertainty and empower ourselves to step confidently into the unknown and seize the opportunity it presents. Applying the following four principles will help you do that.

1. Reframe Your Situation

Most people are loss-averse. Multiple studies demonstrate that the way you frame things affects how you make decisions. The research shows, for instance, that if one treatment for a new disease is described as 95% effective and another as 5% ineffective, people prefer the former even though the two are statistically identical. Every innovation, every change, every transformation—personal or professional—comes with potential upsides and downsides. And though most of us instinctively focus on the latter, it's possible to shift that mindset and decrease our fear.

One of our favorite ways of doing this is the "infinite game" approach, developed by New York University professor James Carse. His advice is to stop seeing the rules, boundaries, and purpose of the "game" you're playing—the job you're after, the project you've been assigned, the career path you're on—as fixed. That puts you in a win-or-lose mentality in which uncertainty heightens your anxiety. In contrast, infinite players recognize uncertainty as an essential part of the game—one that adds an element of surprise and possibility and enables them to challenge their roles and the game's parameters.

Yvon Chouinard, the cofounder of Patagonia, is an infinite player. As a kid he struggled to fit in, running away from one school, almost failing out of a second, and becoming a "dirtbag" climber after he graduated. But rather than seeing himself as a failure, he recounts in his book *Let My People Go Surfing*, he "learned at an early age that it's better to invent your own game; then you can always be a winner."

Chouinard not only created one of the world's most successful outdoor-apparel brands but also changed production norms by adopting more-sustainable materials, altered the retail model by refitting old buildings for new shops, and challenged traditional HR policies by introducing practices like on-site childcare. Some of those innovations created uncertainty for the business. For example, Patagonia adopted organic cotton before it became popular, when it was expensive and hard to source. When a financial downturn hit, outsiders encouraged the company to buy cheaper materials. But using organic cotton was in keeping with its values, so Patagonia persisted, despite the cost and the supply risks, and in the end grew its sales while its competitors saw their sales fall.

Chouinard has learned to face uncertainty with courage—and in fact to be energized by it—because he views his role as improving the game, not just playing it. "Managers of a business that want to be around for the next 100 years had better love change," he advises in his book. "When there [is] no crisis, the wise leader . . . will invent one."

Of course, when uncertainty is forced upon us, we often need help reframing. Consider Amy and Michael, a professional couple with four children who moved from the United States to France in 2017 for Michael's job. When the pandemic started, his position was eliminated, and then companies that initially promised him job offers started stalling. In July 2020, Amy and Michael were scheduled to fly home to the United States, but three days before they left, they still didn't have jobs or even a place to live. Family and friends were asking for updates, and their teenagers harangued them: "You are the worst parents ever! How can you have no clue where we're going next?"

Two days before their flight, Amy confided to us over lunch that Michael had been offered a job, but neither of them wanted him to accept it. "Should we just take the bird in hand?" she wondered aloud. "I feel like we are such losers." We encouraged her to reframe. She and Michael were showing resilience and bravery by exploring all possible next steps and holding out for the right one. How lucky their kids were to have parents bold enough to know what they really wanted and wait for it! The couple returned to the States with curiosity and courage and, by summer's end, had both found jobs they loved as well as a fixer-upper home in a fun location.

2. Prime Yourself for New Risks

Although innovators often talk about eating uncertainty for breakfast, if you dig deeper, you discover some curious habits. When Paul Smith—a designer known for daring color combinations—travels, he always stays in the same hotel, often in the same room. Others we've studied book the same airplane seat for every flight, follow the same morning routine, or wear the same clothes. Steve Jobs had a lifetime supply of black turtlenecks.

All those habits provide balance. By reducing uncertainty in one part of your life, you're primed to tolerate more of it in other parts. Some people ground themselves with steady, long-term relationships, for instance. As the serial entrepreneur Sam Yagan, one of *Time*'s 100 most influential people and the former CEO of Match .com explains, "My best friends are from junior high and high school. I married my high school sweetheart. Given how much ambiguity I traffic in at work, I do look for less in other areas of my life."

You can also prime yourself for uncertainty by getting to know the kinds of risk you have a natural aversion to or an affinity with. Case in point: Back when Nathan was pursuing a PhD in Silicon Valley and Susannah had started a clothing line that wasn't yet making money, we had four children to support and were still living off student loans in a few hundred square feet of on-campus housing. At lunch one day, Nathan told his mentor, Tina Seelig, "Let's face it, if I really had any courage, I would become an entrepreneur, but I'm just not a risk-taker." Tina disagreed. She explained that there are many types of risks: financial, intellectual, social, emotional, physical, and so on. In Nathan's situation, avoiding financial risk by pursuing a stable career as an academic—while still taking intellectual risks—was a prudent choice. The important lesson is that knowing which risks you tolerate well can help you see where to push more boldly into the frontier, while knowing which you don't will help you prepare so that you can approach them with more confidence.

Just as important, you can increase your risk tolerance by taking smaller risks, even in unrelated fields. Consider Piet Coelewij, a former senior executive at

Amazon and Philips. When he was thinking of leaving the corporate track to head the expansion of Sonos—then a startup—in Europe, he decided to take up kickboxing. Coelewij describes himself as "naturally fearful of physical confrontation," but trying kickboxing helped him build up his muscles for dealing with uncertainty, which made him "more comfortable with higher-risk decisions in other settings with less complete information," he says. "Once you are in a cycle of lowering fear and developing courage, you create a virtuous circle that allows you to continuously improve."

3. Do Something

Taking action is one of the most important parts of facing uncertainty, since you learn with each step you take. Research by Timothy Ott and Kathleen Eisenhardt demonstrates that most successful breakthroughs are produced by a series of small steps, not giant bet-the-farm efforts.[1] Starting modestly can be more effective and less anxiety-provoking than trying to do everything at once.

When Jenn Hyman and Jenny Fleiss, the founders of Rent the Runway, first had the idea of renting out designer dresses online, they were students at Harvard Business School. But they didn't begin by writing a business plan, raising money, and then getting big as fast as possible. Instead, they made one small move: They rustled up some dresses, set up a dressing room on Harvard's campus before a big dance, and observed firsthand whether women would rent them. Then, one experiment after another, one step at a time, they built a large, successful public company.

Sometimes you need to quickly ramp up your learning to blow away the fog that obscures the view of what to do next. Entrepreneurs face that challenge all the time. Research on the most effective startup accelerators demonstrates that the best way to help founders meet it is to make them talk with as many people, from as many different backgrounds, as quickly as possible (instead of keeping their ideas to themselves for fear that someone might steal them).[2] Leading accelerators often force entrepreneurs to meet more than 200 people, some from seemingly unrelated backgrounds, in just one month.

It's not unusual for invaluable input to come from unexpected corners. The founder of one new platform dedicated to helping charities, including religious organizations, initially balked at the feedback session his accelerator had arranged with the vice president of marketing at Playboy. To his shock, the VP not only was a churchgoer but also gave him some of the most helpful advice he had received so far.

Finally, as you make your way forward, focus on values rather than on goals. David Heinemeier Hansson, the creator of Ruby on Rails and the cofounder of multiple startups, including Basecamp and Hey.com, views goals as "oppressive" and argues that setting them doesn't even work. "Whether you meet $10 million or not does not happen because you set that as a goal," he explains. If you instead aim to fulfill your values (which for him include coding great software, treating employees well, and acting ethically in the market), you'll have the confidence to make the moves you need to, no matter how the world responds, because you've redefined what success means to you. Even if a big project fails, he says, "I will still look back on the path—the two years and millions of dollars we spent developing this thing—and feel great about it."

He took that approach when Apple began imposing exorbitant app store fees on his most recent project, Hey .com, threatening to shut the new email service down just after it launched. He admits that even he felt anxiety about the uncertainty, just as anyone else would. But his focus on values, rather than goals—in particular, on fairness in the tech industry—"gave us freedom to go all in" fighting back, he says. His situation became a rallying point for entrepreneurs, and the free press that resulted became "the greatest launch campaign we could have imagined."

4. Sustain Yourself

According to Ben Feringa, who won a Nobel Prize in chemistry for work on molecular machines that could one day power nanobots that repair the pipes in your house or keep diseases out of your blood, scientific discovery happens only after facing uncertainty. That means, he says, you have to "get resilient at handling the frustration that comes with it." His approach includes both emotional hygiene (attending to emotions—much as you would a physical wound—so that they don't turn into paralyzing self-doubt or unproductive rumination) and reality checks (in which you recognize that failure is just part of the process).

Feringa admits that failing hurts and that he allows himself to feel frustrated, even for a few days. But then he stops and asks, "What insights can I take away from this?" "What's the next step I can work on?" Whether he realizes it or not, he's adopting one of many lenses that can help people recast setbacks, such as the learning lens (what you can learn from them), the gratitude lens (what you still have, not what you lost), the timing lens (it's just not the right time now, but that doesn't mean it won't ever be), and our favorite: the challenge lens (you become the hero only by facing obstacles).

Another practice that the scientists, creators, and entrepreneurs we've studied use to sustain themselves is to focus on the people and things that have meaning for them. You can get through anything—not just the fear of potential losses but the pain of real ones—by holding tight to what really matters.

Take Jos and Alison Skeates, a British couple who launched a small chain of jewelry shops featuring new designers. They'd opened locations in three London neighborhoods—Clerkenwell, Notting Hill, and Chiswick—all while raising their two young girls. Then a series of disasters struck. First, construction around the Notting Hill store killed foot traffic. Then the financial crisis of 2008 crushed sales and, much worse, Alison was diagnosed with an aggressive form of cancer. They had to close two shops and declare bankruptcy. But they navigated those tragedies by remembering that their love and their family were more important than the business.

Slowly, Alison's health improved, and the cancer went into remission. Eventually they relaunched the Clerkenwell shop, repaid all their former creditors, and even won an award for being the U.K. jewelry boutique of the year. They also discovered a new, more meaningful pursuit: becoming one of the U.K.'s first certified B-corp jewelry workshops, leading the way in sustainable practices.

Ultimately, their switch to sustainable jewelry strengthened them and their business. Recently, Jos went back to school to earn a master's degree in sustainability. More than 30 years out of school, he seriously doubted whether he could meet the rigorous reading and writing demands of the program while still running the store. The upside to this uncertainty? "What I have learned has been so interesting and inspiring, and our sales have increased," he says. Although he and Alison didn't build the chic jewelry empire they had imagined, their lives are happier and richer on this side of many challenges.

Resilience—being able to take a blow and stay standing—is important. But we argue for something more: learning to transform uncertainty into opportunity. The only way for any of us to tap into new possibilities is through the gateway of the unknown. And it doesn't have to be a painful process if you believe in your ability to navigate it. Our hope is that you can use our advice to transform your relationship with change and inspire others to do the same.

Nathan Furr is a professor of strategy at INSEAD and a coauthor of five bestselling books, including *The Upside* *of Uncertainty, The Innovator's Method, Leading Transformation, Innovation Capital,* and *Nail It Then Scale It.*

Susannah Harmon Furr is an entrepreneur based in Paris. She is a coauthor of *The Upside of Uncertainty* (Harvard Business Review Press, 2022).

NOTES

1. Timothy E. Ott and Kathleen M. Eisenhardt, "Decision Weaving: Forming Novel, Complex Strategy in Entrepreneurial Settings," *Strategic Management Journal* 41 (2020): 2275–2314, https://doi.org/10.1002/smj.3189.

2. Susan L. Cohen, Christopher B. Bingham, and Benjamin L. Hallen, "The Role of Accelerator Designs in Mitigating Bounded Rationality in New Ventures," *Administrative Science Quarterly* 64, no. 4 (2019): 810–854, https://doi.org/10.1177/0001839218782131.

Leading Change: Why Transformation Efforts Fail

by John P. Kotter

Editor's note: John P. Kotter is renowned for his work on leading organizational change. This article was originally published in the March–April 1995 issue of HBR and has been one of the publication's bestselling reprints. Though the types and pace of change have varied and accelerated over time, the eight largest errors that doom transformational change remain challenges for today's leaders. As you're moving forward with change, keep these time-tested tenets in mind.

Over the past decade, I have watched more than 100 companies try to remake themselves into significantly better competitors. They have included large organizations (Ford) and small ones (Landmark Communications), companies based in the United States (General Motors) and elsewhere (British Airways), corporations that were on their knees (Eastern Airlines), and companies that were earning good money (Bristol-Myers Squibb). These efforts have gone under many banners: total quality management, reengineering, rightsizing, restructuring, cultural change, and turnaround. But, in almost every case, the basic goal has been the same: to make fundamental changes in how business is conducted in order to help cope with a new, more challenging market environment.

A few of these corporate change efforts have been very successful. A few have been utter failures. Most fall somewhere in between, with a distinct tilt toward the lower end of the scale. The lessons that can be drawn are interesting and will probably be relevant to even more organizations in the increasingly competitive business environment of the coming decade.

The most general lesson to be learned from the more successful cases is that the change process goes through a series of phases that, in total, usually require a considerable length of time. Skipping steps creates only the illusion of speed and never produces a satisfying result. A second very general lesson is that critical mistakes in any of the phases can have a devastating impact, slowing momentum and negating hard-won gains. Perhaps because we have relatively little experience in renewing organizations, even very capable people often make at least one big error.

EIGHT STEPS TO TRANSFORMING YOUR ORGANIZATION

1. Establish a sense of urgency.

    - Examine market and competitive realities.

    - Identify and discuss crises, potential crises, or major opportunities.

2. Form a powerful guiding coalition.

    - Assemble a group with enough power to lead the change effort.

    - Encourage the group to work together as a team.

3. Create a vision.

    - Create a vision to help direct the change effort.

    - Develop strategies for achieving that vision.

4. Communicate the vision.

    - Use every vehicle possible to communicate the new vision and strategies.

    - Teach new behaviors by the example of the guiding coalition.

5. Empower others to act on the vision.

    - Get rid of obstacles to change.

    - Change systems or structures that seriously undermine the vision.

                                        (continued)

EIGHT STEPS TO TRANSFORMING YOUR ORGANIZATION

- Encourage risk-taking and nontraditional ideas, activities, and actions.

6. Plan for and create short-term wins.

   - Plan for visible performance improvements.

   - Create those improvements.

   - Recognize and reward employees involved in the improvements.

7. Consolidate improvements and produce still more change.

   - Use increased credibility to change systems, structures, and policies that don't fit the vision.

   - Hire, promote, and develop employees who can implement the vision.

   - Reinvigorate the process with new projects, themes, and change agents.

8. Institutionalize new approaches.

   - Articulate the connections between the new behaviors and corporate success.

   - Develop the means to ensure leadership development and succession.

Error 1: Not Establishing a Great Enough Sense of Urgency

Most successful change efforts begin when some individuals or some groups start to look hard at a company's competitive situation, market position, technological trends, and financial performance. They focus on the potential revenue drop when an important patent expires, the five-year trend in declining margins in a core business, or an emerging market that everyone seems to be ignoring. They then find ways to communicate this information broadly and dramatically, especially with respect to crises, potential crises, or great opportunities that are very timely. This first step is essential because just getting a transformation program started requires the aggressive cooperation of many individuals. Without motivation, people won't help, and the effort goes nowhere.

Compared with other steps in the change process, phase one can sound easy. It is not. Well over 50% of the companies I have watched fail in this first phase. What are the reasons for that failure? Sometimes executives underestimate how hard it can be to drive people out of their comfort zones. Sometimes they grossly overestimate how successful they have already been in increasing urgency. Sometimes they lack patience: "Enough with the preliminaries; let's get on with it." In many cases, executives become paralyzed by the downside possibilities. They worry that employees with seniority will become defensive, that morale will drop, that events will spin out of control, that short-term business results will be jeopardized, that the stock will sink, and that they will be blamed for creating a crisis.

A paralyzed senior management often comes from having too many managers and not enough leaders. Management's mandate is to minimize risk and to keep the current system operating. Change, by definition, requires creating a new system, which in turn always demands leadership. Phase one in a renewal process typically goes nowhere until enough real leaders are promoted or hired into senior-level jobs.

Transformations often begin, and begin well, when an organization has a new head who is a good leader and who sees the need for a major change. If the renewal target is the entire company, the CEO is key. If change is needed in a division, the division general manager is key. When these individuals are not new leaders, great leaders, or change champions, phase one can be a huge challenge.

Bad business results are both a blessing and a curse in the first phase. On the positive side, losing money does catch people's attention. But it also gives less maneuvering room. With good business results, the opposite is true: Convincing people of the need for change is much harder, but you have more resources to help make changes.

But whether the starting point is good performance or bad, in the more successful cases I have witnessed, an individual or a group always facilitates a frank discussion of potentially unpleasant facts about new competition, shrinking margins, decreasing market share, flat earnings, a lack of revenue growth, or other relevant indices of a declining competitive position. Because there seems to be an almost universal human tendency to shoot the bearer of bad news, especially if the head of the organization is not a change champion, executives in these companies often rely on outsiders to bring unwanted information. Wall Street analysts, customers, and consultants can all be helpful in this regard. The purpose of all this activity, in the words of one former CEO of a large European company, is "to make the status quo seem more dangerous than launching into the unknown."

In a few of the most successful cases, a group has manufactured a crisis. One CEO deliberately engineered the largest accounting loss in the company's history, creating huge pressures from Wall Street in the process. One division president commissioned first-ever customer satisfaction surveys, knowing full well that the results would be terrible. He then made these findings public. On the surface, such moves can look unduly risky. But there is also risk in playing it too safe: When the urgency rate is not pumped up enough, the transformation process cannot succeed, and the long-term future of the organization is put in jeopardy.

When is the urgency rate high enough? From what I have seen, the answer is when about 75% of a company's management is honestly convinced that business as usual is totally unacceptable. Anything less can produce very serious problems later on in the process.

Error 2: Not Creating a Powerful Enough Guiding Coalition

Major renewal programs often start with just one or two people. In cases of successful transformation efforts, the leadership coalition grows and grows over time. But whenever some minimum mass is not achieved early in the effort, nothing much worthwhile happens.

It is often said that major change is impossible unless the head of the organization is an active supporter. What I am talking about goes far beyond that. In successful transformations, the chairman or president or division general manager, plus another five or 15 or 50 people, come together and develop a shared commitment to excellent performance through renewal. In my experience, this group never includes all of the company's most senior executives because some people just won't buy in, at least not at first. But in the most successful cases, the coalition is always pretty powerful—in terms of titles, information and expertise, reputations, and relationships.

In both small and large organizations, a successful guiding team may consist of only three to five people during the first year of a renewal effort. But in big companies, the coalition needs to grow to the 20 to 50 range before much progress can be made in phase three and beyond. Senior managers always form the core of the group. But sometimes you find board members, a representative from a key customer, or even a powerful union leader.

Because the guiding coalition includes members who are not part of senior management, it tends to operate outside of the normal hierarchy by definition. This can be awkward, but it is clearly necessary. If the existing hierarchy were working well, there would be no need for a major transformation. But since the current system is not working, reform generally demands activity outside of formal boundaries, expectations, and protocol.

A high sense of urgency within the managerial ranks helps enormously in putting a guiding coalition together. But more is usually required. Someone needs to get these people together, help them develop a shared assessment of their company's problems and opportunities, and create a minimum level of trust and communication. Off-site retreats, for two or three days, are one popular vehicle for accomplishing this task. I have seen many groups of five to 35 executives attend a series of these retreats over a period of months.

Companies that fail in phase two usually underestimate the difficulties of producing change and thus the importance of a powerful guiding coalition. Sometimes they have no history of teamwork at the top and therefore undervalue the importance of this type of coalition. Sometimes they expect the team to be led by a staff executive from human resources, quality, or strategic planning instead of a key line manager. No matter how capable or dedicated the staff head, groups without strong line leadership never achieve the power that is required.

Efforts that don't have a powerful enough guiding coalition can make apparent progress for a while. But, sooner or later, the opposition gathers itself together and stops the change.

Error 3: Lacking a Vision

In every successful transformation effort that I have seen, the guiding coalition develops a picture of the future that is relatively easy to communicate and appeals to customers, stockholders, and employees. A vision always goes beyond the numbers that are typically found in five-year plans. A vision says something that helps clarify the direction in which an organization needs to move. Sometimes the first draft comes mostly from a single individual. It is usually a bit blurry, at least initially. But after the coalition works at it for three or five or even 12 months, something much better emerges through their tough analytical thinking and a little dreaming. Eventually, a strategy for achieving that vision is also developed.

In one midsize European company, the first pass at a vision contained two-thirds of the basic ideas that were in the final product. The concept of global reach was in the initial version from the beginning. So was the idea of becoming preeminent in certain businesses. But one central idea in the final version—getting out of low value-added activities—came only after a series of discussions over a period of several months.

Without a sensible vision, a transformation effort can easily dissolve into a list of confusing and incompatible projects that can take the organization in the wrong direction or nowhere at all. Without a sound vision, the reengineering project in the accounting department, the new 360-degree performance appraisal from the human resources department, the plant's quality program, the cultural change project in the sales force will not add up in a meaningful way.

In failed transformations, you often find plenty of plans, directives, and programs but no vision. In one case, a company gave out four-inch-thick notebooks describing its change effort. In mind-numbing detail, the books spelled out procedures, goals, methods, and deadlines. But nowhere was there a clear and compelling statement of where all this was leading. Not surprisingly, most of the employees with whom I talked were either confused or alienated. The big, thick books did not rally them together or inspire change. In fact, they probably had just the opposite effect.

In a few of the less successful cases that I have seen, management had a sense of direction, but it was too complicated or blurry to be useful. Recently, I asked an executive in a midsize company to describe his vision and received in return a barely comprehensible 30-minute lecture. Buried in his answer were the basic elements of a sound vision. But they were buried—deeply.

A useful rule of thumb: If you can't communicate the vision to someone in five minutes or less and get a reaction that signifies both understanding and interest, you are not yet done with this phase of the transformation process.

Error 4: Undercommunicating the Vision by a Factor of Ten

I've seen three patterns with respect to communication, all very common. In the first, a group actually does develop a pretty good transformation vision and then proceeds to communicate it by holding a single meeting or sending out a single communication. Having used about 0.0001% of the yearly intracompany communication, the group is startled when few people seem to understand the new approach. In the second pattern, the head of the organization spends a considerable amount of time making speeches to employee groups, but most people still don't get it (not surprising, since vision captures only 0.0005% of the total yearly communication). In the third pattern, much more effort goes into newsletters and speeches, but some very visible senior executives still behave in ways that are antithetical to the vision. The net result is that cynicism among the troops goes up, while belief in the communication goes down.

Transformation is impossible unless hundreds or thousands of people are willing to help, often to the point of making short-term sacrifices. Employees will not make sacrifices, even if they are unhappy with the status quo, unless they believe that useful change is possible. Without credible communication, and a lot of it, the hearts and minds of the troops are never captured.

This fourth phase is particularly challenging if the short-term sacrifices include job losses. Gaining understanding and support is tough when downsizing is a part of the vision. For this reason, successful visions usually include new growth possibilities and the commitment to treat fairly anyone who is laid off.

Executives who communicate well incorporate messages into their hour-by-hour activities. In a routine discussion about a business problem, they talk about how proposed solutions fit (or don't fit) into the bigger picture. In a regular performance appraisal, they talk about how the employee's behavior helps or undermines the vision. In a review of a division's quarterly performance, they talk not only about the numbers but also about how the division's executives are contributing to the transformation. In a routine Q&A with employees at a company facility, they tie their answers back to renewal goals.

In more successful transformation efforts, executives use all existing communication channels to broadcast the vision. They turn boring, unread company newsletters into lively articles about the vision. They take ritualistic, tedious quarterly management meetings and turn them into exciting discussions of the transformation. They throw out much of the company's generic management education and replace it with courses that focus on business problems and the new vision. The guiding principle is simple: Use every possible channel, especially those that are being wasted on nonessential information.

Perhaps even more important, most of the executives I have known in successful cases of major change learn to "walk the talk." They consciously attempt to become a living symbol of the new corporate culture. This is often not easy. A 60-year-old plant manager who has spent precious little time over 40 years thinking about customers will not suddenly behave in a customer-oriented way. But I have witnessed just such a person change, and change a great deal. In that case, a high level of urgency helped. The fact that the man was a part of the guiding coalition and the vision-creation team also helped. So did all the communication, which kept reminding him of the desired behavior, and all the feedback from his peers and subordinates, which helped him see when he was not engaging in that behavior.

Communication comes in both words and deeds, and the latter are often the most powerful form. Nothing undermines change more than behavior by important individuals that is inconsistent with their words.

Error 5: Not Removing Obstacles to the New Vision

Successful transformations begin to involve large numbers of people as the process progresses. Employees are emboldened to try new approaches, to develop new ideas, and to provide leadership. The only constraint is that the actions fit within the broad parameters of the overall vision. The more people involved, the better the outcome.

To some degree, a guiding coalition empowers others to take action simply by successfully communicating the new direction. But communication is never sufficient by itself. Renewal also requires the removal of obstacles. Too often, an employee understands the new vision and wants to help make it happen, but an elephant appears to be blocking the path. In some cases, the elephant is in the person's head, and the challenge is to convince the individual that no external obstacle exists. But in most cases, the blockers are very real.

Sometimes the obstacle is the organizational structure: Narrow job categories can seriously undermine efforts to increase productivity or make it very difficult even to think about customers. Sometimes compensation or performance-appraisal systems make people choose between the new vision and their own self-interest. Perhaps worst of all are bosses who refuse to change and who make demands that are inconsistent with the overall effort.

One company began its transformation process with much publicity and actually made good progress through the fourth phase. Then the change effort ground to a halt because the officer in charge of the company's largest division was allowed to undermine most of the new initiatives. He paid lip service to the process but did not change his behavior or encourage his managers to change. He did not reward the unconventional ideas called for in the vision. He allowed human resource systems to remain intact even when they were clearly inconsistent with the new ideals. I think the officer's motives were complex. To some degree, he did not believe the company needed major change. To some degree, he felt personally threatened by all the change. To some degree, he was afraid that he could not produce both change and the expected operating profit. But despite the fact that they backed the renewal effort, the other officers did virtually nothing to stop the one blocker. Again, the reasons were complex. The company had no history of confronting problems like this. Some people were afraid of the officer. The CEO was concerned that he might lose a talented executive. The net result was disastrous. Lower-level managers concluded that senior management had lied to them about their commitment to renewal, cynicism grew, and the whole effort collapsed.

In the first half of a transformation, no organization has the momentum, power, or time to get rid of all obstacles. But the big ones must be confronted and removed. If the blocker is a person, it is important that he or she be treated fairly and in a way that is consistent with the new vision. Action is essential, both to empower others and to maintain the credibility of the change effort as a whole.

Error 6: Not Systematically Planning for, and Creating, Short-Term Wins

Real transformation takes time, and a renewal effort risks losing momentum if there are no short-term goals to meet and celebrate. Most people won't go on the long march unless they see compelling evidence in 12 to 24 months that the journey is producing expected results. Without short-term wins, too many people give up or actively join the ranks of those people who have been resisting change.

One to two years into a successful transformation effort, you find quality beginning to go up on certain indices or the decline in net income stopping. You find some successful new product introductions or an upward shift in market share. You find an impressive productivity improvement or a statistically higher customer satisfaction rating. But whatever the case, the win is unambiguous. The result is not just a judgment call that can be discounted by those opposing change.

Creating short-term wins is different from hoping for short-term wins. The latter is passive, the former active. In a successful transformation, managers actively look for ways to obtain clear performance improvements, establish goals in the yearly planning system, achieve the objectives, and reward the people involved with recognition, promotions, and even money. For example, the guiding coalition at a U.S. manufacturing company produced a highly visible and successful new product introduction about 20 months after the start of its renewal effort. The new product was selected about six months into the effort because it met multiple criteria: It could be designed and launched in a relatively short period, it could be handled by a small team of people who were devoted to the new vision, it had upside potential, and the new product-development team could operate outside the established departmental structure without practical problems. Little was left to chance, and the win boosted the credibility of the renewal process.

Managers often complain about being forced to produce short-term wins, but I've found that pressure can be a useful element in a change effort. When it becomes clear to people that major change will take a long time, urgency levels can drop. Commitments to produce short-term wins help keep the urgency level up and force detailed analytical thinking that can clarify or revise visions.

Error 7: Declaring Victory Too Soon

After a few years of hard work, managers may be tempted to declare victory with the first clear performance improvement. While celebrating a win is fine, declaring the war won can be catastrophic. Until changes sink deeply into a company's culture, a process that can take five to ten years, new approaches are fragile and subject to regression.

In the recent past, I have watched a dozen change efforts operate under the reengineering theme. In all but two cases, victory was declared and the expensive consultants were paid and thanked when the first major project was completed after two to three years. Within two more years, the useful changes that had been introduced slowly disappeared. In two of the ten cases, it's hard to find any trace of the reengineering work today.

Over the past 20 years, I've seen the same sort of thing happen to huge quality projects, organizational development efforts, and more. Typically, the problems start early in the process: The urgency level is not intense enough, the guiding coalition is not powerful enough, and the vision is not clear enough. But it is the premature victory celebration that kills momentum. And then the powerful forces associated with tradition take over.

Ironically, it is often a combination of change initiators and change resisters that creates the premature victory celebration. In their enthusiasm over a clear sign of progress, the initiators go overboard. They are then joined by resisters, who are quick to spot any opportunity to stop change. After the celebration is over, the resisters point to the victory as a sign that the war has been won and the troops should be sent home. Weary troops allow themselves to be convinced that they won. Once home, the foot soldiers are reluctant to climb back on the ships. Soon thereafter, change comes to a halt, and tradition creeps back in.

Instead of declaring victory, leaders of successful efforts use the credibility afforded by short-term wins to tackle even bigger problems. They go after systems and structures that are not consistent with the transformation vision and have not been confronted before. They pay great attention to who is promoted, who is hired, and how people are developed. They include new reengineering projects that are even bigger in scope than the initial ones. They understand that renewal efforts take not months but years. In fact, in one of the most success-ful transformations that I have ever seen, we quantified the amount of change that occurred each year over a seven-year period. On a scale of one (low) to ten (high), year one received a two, year two a four, year three a three, year four a seven, year five an eight, year six a four, and year seven a two. The peak came in year five, fully 36 months after the first set of visible wins.

Error 8: Not Anchoring Changes in the Corporation's Culture

In the final analysis, change sticks when it becomes "the way we do things around here," when it seeps into the bloodstream of the corporate body. Until new behaviors are rooted in social norms and shared values, they are subject to degradation as soon as the pressure for change is removed.

Two factors are particularly important in institution-alizing change in corporate culture. The first is a con-scious attempt to show people how the new approaches, behaviors, and attitudes have helped improve perfor-mance. When people are left on their own to make the connections, they sometimes create very inaccurate links. For example, because results improved while char-ismatic Harry was boss, the troops link his mostly idio-syncratic style with those results instead of seeing how their own improved customer service and productivity were instrumental. Helping people see the right con-nections requires communication. Indeed, one company was relentless, and it paid off enormously. Time was spent at every major management meeting to discuss why performance was increasing. The company newspaper ran article after article showing how changes had boosted earnings.

The second factor is taking sufficient time to make sure that the next generation of top management really does personify the new approach. If the requirements for promotion don't change, renewal rarely lasts. One bad succession decision at the top of an organization can undermine a decade of hard work. Poor succession decisions are possible when boards of directors are not an integral part of the renewal effort. In at least three instances I have seen, the champion for change was the retiring executive, and although his successor was not a resister he was not a change champion. Because the boards did not understand the transformations in any detail, they could not see that their choices were not good fits. The retiring executive in one case tried unsuccessfully to talk his board into a less seasoned candidate who better personified the transformation. In the other two cases, the CEOs did not resist the boards' choices, because they felt the transformation could not be undone by their successors. They were wrong. Within two years, signs of renewal began to disappear at both companies.

There are still more mistakes that people make, but these eight are the big ones. I realize that in a short article everything is made to sound a bit too simplistic. In reality, even successful change efforts are messy and full of surprises. But just as a relatively simple vision is needed to guide people through a major change, so a vision of the change process can reduce the error rate. And fewer errors can spell the difference between success and failure.

———————

John P. Kotter is a bestselling author, award-winning business and management thought leader, business entrepreneur, and the Konosuke Matsushita Professor of Leadership, Emeritus, at Harvard Business School. His ideas, books, and company, Kotter International, help people lead organizations in an era of increasingly rapid change. He is a coauthor of the book *Change*, which details how leaders can leverage challenges and opportunities to make sustainable workplace changes in a rapidly accelerating world.

Index

Index

Index

Index

Smart advice and inspiration from a source you trust.

If you enjoyed this book and want more comprehensive guidance on essential professional skills, turn to the HBR Guides Boxed Set. Packed with the practical advice you need to succeed, this seven-volume collection provides smart answers to your most pressing work challenges, from writing more effective emails and delivering persuasive presentations to setting priorities and managing up and across.

Harvard Business Review Guides

Available in paperback or ebook format. Plus, find downloadable tools and templates to help you get started.

- Better Business Writing
- Building Your Business Case
- Buying a Small Business
- Coaching Employees
- Delivering Effective Feedback
- Finance Basics for Managers
- Getting the Mentoring You Need
- Getting the Right Work Done

- Leading Teams
- Making Every Meeting Matter
- Managing Stress at Work
- Managing Up and Across
- Negotiating
- Office Politics
- Persuasive Presentations
- Project Management

Notes

Notes

Notes

Notes

Notes

Notes

Notes

Notes

Notes